Digital Audio Editing Fundamentals

Wallace Jackson

Apress®

Digital Audio Editing Fundamentals

Wallace Jackson
Lompoc, California, USA

ISBN 978-1-4842-1647-7
DOI 10.1007/978-1-4842-1648-4

ISBN 978-1-4842-1648-4 (eBook)

Library of Congress Control Number: 2015958667

    Managing Director: Welmoed Spahr
    Lead Editor: Steve Anglin
    Technical Reviewer: Chád Darby
    Editorial Board: Steve Anglin, Louise Corrigan, Jonathan Gennick, Robert Hutchinson, Michelle Lowman, James Markham, Susan McDermott, Matthew Moodie, Jeffrey Pepper, Douglas Pundick, Ben Renow-Clarke, Gwenan Spearing, Steve Weiss
    Coordinating Editor: Mark Powers
    Copy Editor: Kim Burton-Weisman
    Compositor: SPi Global
    Indexer: SPi Global
    Artist: SPi Global

Distributed to the book trade worldwide by Springer Science+Business Media New York, 233 Spring Street, 6th Floor, New York, NY 10013. Phone 1-800-SPRINGER, fax (201) 348-4505, e-mail orders-ny@springer-sbm.com, or visit www.springeronline.com. Apress Media, LLC is a California LLC and the sole member (owner) is Springer Science + Business Media Finance Inc (SSBM Finance Inc). SSBM Finance Inc is a **Delaware** corporation.

For information on translations, please e-mail rights@apress.com, or visit www.apress.com.

Apress and friends of ED books may be purchased in bulk for academic, corporate, or promotional use. eBook versions and licenses are also available for most titles. For more information, reference our Special Bulk Sales–eBook Licensing web page at www.apress.com/bulk-sales.

Any source code or other supplementary materials referenced by the author in this text are available to readers at www.apress.com/9781484216477. For detailed information about how to locate your book's source code, go to www.apress.com/source-code/. Readers can also access source code at SpringerLink in the Supplementary Material section for each chapter.

Printed on acid-free paper

Digital Audio Editing Fundamentals is dedicated to everyone in the open source community who is working so diligently to make professional application development software and content development tools freely available to rich application developers so that they can utilize them to achieve our creative dreams and financial goals. Last but not least, I dedicate this book to my father, Parker Jackson, my family, my life-long friends, and my production ranch neighbors for their constant help, assistance, and those relaxing, late-night BBQs!

Contents at a Glance

Contents

About the Author

Wallace Jackson has been writing for several leading multimedia publications about work in the new media content development industry, after contributing a piece about advanced-computer-processing architectures for the centerfold (a removable "mini-issue" insert) of an original issue of *AV Video Multimedia Producer* magazine that was distributed at the SIGGRAPH trade show. Wallace has written for a large number of popular publications about his work in interactive 3D and new-media-advertising campaign design, including *3DArtist* magazine, *Desktop Publisher Journal*, *CrossMedia* magazine, *Kiosk* magazine, *AV Video Multimedia Producer* magazine, *Digital Signage* magazine, and many other publications.

Wallace has authored a dozen Apress book titles, including four titles in its popular Pro Android series, Java and JavaFX game development titles, digital-image-compositing titles, and new-media-content-production titles.

In the current book on digital image compositing, he focuses on the GIMP and Photoshop CS6 digital-image-compositing software packages, and uses them to demonstrate digital-image-editing and -compositing fundamentals to beginners who wish to become digital imaging professionals.

Wallace is currently the CEO of MindTaffy Design, an agency specializing in new media content production and digital campaign design and development, located in Northern Santa Barbara County, halfway between its clientele in Silicon Valley to the north and Hollywood, the "OC," West LA, and San Diego to the south.

MindTaffy Design has created open-source, technology-based (HTML5, JavaScript, Java, JavaFX, and Android 5.3) digital-new-media i3D content deliverables for more than a quarter century (since 1991).

The company's clients consist of a significant number of international branded manufacturers, including Sony, Tyco, Samsung, IBM, Dell, Epson, Nokia, TEAC, Sun Microsystems, Micron, SGI, KDS USA, EIZO, CTX International, KFC, Nanao USA, Techmedia, EZC, and Mitsubishi.

Wallace received his undergraduate BA degree in business economics from the University of California at Los Angeles (UCLA) and his graduate degree in MIS business information systems design and implementation from University of Southern California in Los Angeles (USC). Wallace also received a postgraduate degree in marketing strategy from USC and completed the USC Graduate Entrepreneurship Program. He earned the two USC degrees while at USC's nighttime Marshall School of Business MBA Program, which allowed him to work full time as a COBOL programmer while completing his degrees.

About the Technical Reviewer

Chád ("Shod") Darby is an author, instructor, and speaker in the Java development world. As a recognized authority on Java applications and architectures, he has presented technical sessions at software development conferences worldwide (in the United States, the United Kingdom, India, Russia, and Australia). In his 15 years as a professional software architect, he's had the opportunity to work for Blue Cross/Blue Shield, Merck, Boeing, Red Hat, and a handful of start-up companies.

Chád is a contributing author to several Java books, including *Professional Java E-Commerce* (Wrox Press), *Beginning Java Networking* (Wrox Press), and *XML and Web Services Unleashed* (Sams Publishing). Chád has Java certifications from Sun Microsystems and IBM. He holds a BS in computer science from Carnegie Mellon University.

You can visit Chád's blog at www.luv2code.com to view his free video tutorials on Java. You can also follow him on Twitter at @darbyluvs2code.

Acknowledgments

I would like to acknowledge all of my fantastic editors and their support staff at Apress, who worked those long hours, and who toiled so very hard on this book, to make it the ultimate digital audio editing and compositing fundamentals book title currently in the marketplace.

I would like to specifically thank the following people:

Steve Anglin for his work as the acquisitions editor for the book and for recruiting me to write development titles at Apress covering widely popular open source content-development platforms (Android, Java, JavaFX, HTML5, CSS3, JS, GIMP, etc.).

Matthew Moodie for his work as the development editor on the book, and for his experience and guidance during the process of making the book one of the leading digital audio compositing titles.

Mark Powers for his work as the coordinating editor for the book, and for his constant diligence in making sure that I either hit my chapter delivery deadlines or far surpassed them.

Kim Burton-Weisman for her work as the copy editor on this book, for her careful attention to minute details, and for conforming the text to current Apress book writing standards.

Chád Darby for his work as the technical reviewer on the book and for making sure that I didn't make technical mistakes.

Finally, I'd like to acknowledge Oracle for acquiring Sun Microsystems and continuing to enhance Java and JavaFX, which allows their Java and JavaFX to remain the premiere open-source programming languages, and allows digital audio compositing pipelines to be written in Java code, taking this industry to the next level.

Introduction

Digital audio is currently exploding into the marketplace due to a couple of important market phenomena. The first is HD Audio, which features 24-bit, 96 kHz quality levels, and the second is a proliferation of consumer electronics genres that leverage digital audio specifically. These include digital automobile dashboards that run apps, iTVs that feature both HD and UHD high-definition screens and high-quality digital audio, home appliance devices, remote home control devices, drones, robots, affordable gaming consoles, interactive set-top boxes, digital home theater systems, home media centers, and similar new gadgetry that includes high-quality digital audio, which is what this book is all about. Of course, I will also cover your standard PCs, laptops, tablets, smartphones, e-book readers, notebooks, and netbooks that currently populate the marketplace today.

Digital Audio Editing Fundamentals was intended for HTML5 web site developers, multimedia producers, Android 6 application developers, HTML5 application developers, Java and JavaFX application developers, social media entrepreneurs, podcasters, digital audio user-interface designers, digital audio user-experience designers, or social media users of audio-centric web sites such as SoundCloud, Dubbler, Eevzdrop, DigiSocial, and MySpace. In fact, just about anyone who is interested in generating high-quality, digital audio music, vocals, or other audio assets, such as special effects, delivered using popular MPEG-4, FLAC, Ogg Vorbis, WAV, AIFF, AMR, or MP3 digital audio file formats, will be interested in this *Digital Audio Editing Fundamentals* book.

This book covers digital audio editing and compositing. In the early chapters, this equates to fundamentals: terms, topics, concepts, and definitions. Every subsequent chapter builds upon the knowledge of the previous chapter, so the editing chapters in the book have readers creating advanced digital audio editing moves, using audio filters, analysis tools, and algorithms to apply special effects, create tracks, and the like.

There's even coverage at the end of this book regarding digital audio data footprint optimization, as well as creating digital audio compositing pipelines using open source platforms such as Java 8, JavaFX, HTML5, CSS3, JavaScript, Nyquist 3, and Android Studio 2.0, as well as information covering platforms and consumer electronics devices.

This digital audio fundamentals title will bring you from someone who has no real knowledge of how analog audio or digital audio works, much less how to bridge the two, to teach you about the history, concepts, and algorithms that encompass digital audio.

Chapter 1 focuses on a foundation of digital audio—the sound wave—and makes sure that you have a professional digital audio editing and compositing software package called Audacity 2.1.1 installed on your multimedia production workstation.

Chapter 2 covers the fascinating history of digital audio and the emergence of digital audio on personal computer systems with the advent of MIDI keyboards. MIDI stands for Musical Instrument Digital Interface, and you will see how it worked with synthesizer keyboards, and later sampling keyboards, until powerful modern-day sound design workstations and digital audio editors finally came into their own.

Chapter 3 covers audio data sampling, allowing the reproduction of highly accurate digital audio samples. You will learn about sample resolution and sampling frequency, as well as the mathematics of digital audio and how to use Audacity 2.1 to record your own digital audio sample data.

Chapter 4 covers digital audio transmission and the data formats that are used to stream and to play digital audio over the Internet, as well as in multimedia application development using platforms such as Android Studio, Java 8, or JavaFX, and HTML5 operating systems, such as Google's Chrome OS, Mozilla Firefox OS, Canonical Ubuntu Touch OS, Jolla Sailfish OS, Opera OS, and Tizen OS.

Chapter 5 covers the clean-up of digital audio using noise removal algorithms, as this is the first step that you want to take in your sample recording and editing work process to remove background noise and hiss, and all the extra data footprint the hiss and noise brings along.

Chapter 6 covers digital audio editor tools, including Audacity 2.1 Trimming tools, Data Selection tools, Alignment tools, and real-time audio data preview tools, such as the Digital Audio Scrubbing tools. This chapter gets you closer to the core Audacity editing tools.

Chapter 7 gets into the more manual labor (by not using any algorithms, which do editing "moves" for you). I call it "sample surgery" for fine-tuning your digital audio editing work process and for removing artifacts within your digital audio data samples, whether they are outside of your waveforms (manual editing) or an integrated part of a waveform (algorithmic editing).

Chapter 8 covers the automation of audio editing work using digital audio editing algorithms. Audacity allows hundreds of these algorithms to be added to your toolset by using plug-ins that you can download and install from the Internet. You can add processing power to your digital audio editing software any time that you feel like it.

Chapter 9 uncovers the visualization of digital audio sample data using Audacity spectral analysis tools, which use the Nyquist 3 programming language, so that more of these spectral analysis tools can be added to Audacity 2.1 using the plug-in architecture.

Chapter 10 discusses Audacity 2.1's capabilities in creating digital audio compositing pipelines using the Tracks feature, which is like the Layers feature found in digital image compositing software like GIMP 2.8 and Adobe Photoshop CS6. Audacity 2.1 Tracks allow you to layer your digital audio assets to create a complex digital audio asset creation pipeline.

Chapter 11 gets into the fascinating area of digital audio synthesis through usage of Nyquist Generator plug-ins, which I show you how to load into Audacity using Internet search. I double the amount of synthesizers in Audacity during this fun and informative chapter, making the digital audio editing software even more powerful than it is already.

Chapter 12 covers audio data footprint optimization and what the work process should be to see how much system memory your digital audio samples require, as well as how to ascertain which digital audio codec and data format is the optimal one to utilize for your multimedia production purposes.

Chapter 13 covers how all open source computer programming languages factor into digital audio compositing, both inside of Audacity 2.1.1, as well as with popular open source content delivery platforms, such as Java 8, JavaFX 8, Android Studio 2.0, HTML5, CSS3, and JavaScript, and Amazon Kindle Fire and EPUB 3 for e-book content publishing.

Chapter 14 covers content publishing platforms that support popular digital audio data formats. It also covers the different consumer electronics devices that support digital audio, including those that are most likely to support HD digital audio formats.

If you are interested in digital audio editing, synthesis, sampling, or sound design, and you want to learn the fundamentals and how everything works in the digital domain—from analog sound waves, to MIDI, to synthesis, to navigating a digital audio compositing pipeline, to special effects, to audio data spectral analysis, then this is book for you. Although it is a "fundamentals" book, it covers quite a lot of detail regarding a large spectrum (no pun intended) of digital audio concepts, work processes, terminology, content platforms, digital audio data formats, open programming languages, and digital audio content publishing opportunities.

Chock full of tips, tricks, editing tools, topics, concepts, terminology, techniques, algorithms, and work processes, this *Digital Audio Editing Fundamentals* book can help you to transition from a digital audio editing amateur to the knowledgeable digital audio synthesis, sound design, and audio compositing professional that you seek to become. Improve your digital audio editing, special effects, spectral analysis, and compositing production skills today using this complete, yet concise fundamentals title.

CHAPTER 1

■ ■ ■

The Foundation of Digital Audio: The Sound Wave

Welcome to *Digital Audio Editing Fundamentals*! This book takes you through the foundation of digital audio, as well as manual and algorithmic data sample editing. I start with the lowest-level concepts—in this chapter it's the **sound wave**—and build upon each of these concepts in subsequent chapters until you have a comprehensive understanding of digital audio editing concepts, terminology, audio file formats, work flows, waveform editing, effects processing, and data footprint optimization.

I show you what these concepts, techniques, and terms look like using the most popular digital audio editing software package—open source Audacity 2.1.1, which just so happens to be free for commercial use.

For this reason, the first part of the chapter covers exactly how to download and install Audacity 2.1.1—just in case you don't currently own any digital audio editing software packages. After this, you learn about the foundational element of digital audio editing, which the industry professionals call a **waveform** or a **sample**. Once you put one together with other waveforms, your new media result comprises what's called **digital audio content**.

This book is all about the way your audio waveform samples are edited and processed. Each chapter builds on knowledge from the preceding chapters, until you understand the digital audio sample editing work process.

Downloading and Installing Audacity

You need to have digital audio editing software of one type or another, whether it is Avid ProTools, Cakewalk SONAR, or Propellerhead Reason. If you do not own any of these, you can use the free-for-commercial-use Audacity. Let's install Audacity and free audio encoders.

AudacityTeam.org: Get Your Audacity 2.1 Software

To download Audacity 2.1.1, which is the current stable version, go to **www.audacityteam.org** and click the **Download Audacity 2.1.1** link (see Figure 1-1), or alternately, click the **Download** tab, which is directly underneath the Audacity logo.

© Wallace Jackson 2015
W. Jackson, *Digital Audio Editing Fundamentals*, DOI 10.1007/978-1-4842-1648-4_1

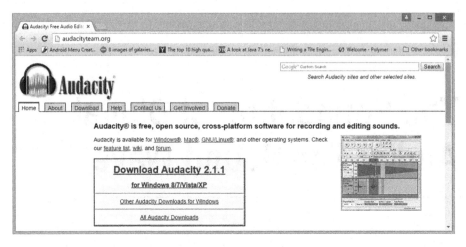

Figure 1-1. *Go to the audacityteam.org site and click Download*

Download the **audacity-win-2.1.1.exe** installer file if you are using Windows (otherwise, the Linux or Mac version) and then double-click it to start your installation process. Audacity for Windows is a 32-bit version; if you want to run 64-bit Audacity, use Linux.

Once the installation starts, select the language that you want to use for your audio editing (I chose English), and then click the **OK** button (see Figure 1-2).

Figure 1-2. *Select the language for the install*

After you click the OK button, you see the **Welcome to the Audacity Setup Wizard** dialog. Click **Next** to continue.

Review the GNU license information (see the right screen in Figure 1-3) and then click the **Next** button.

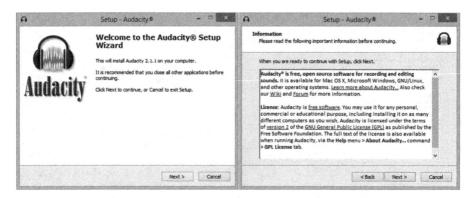

Figure 1-3. *Click Next to read GNU licensing information*

I recommend that you use the destination location default specified by the installer—C:\Program Files (x86)\Audacity—since that is where the third-party products compatible with Audacity will look for the software on your computer system. Click **Next**. Select **Create a desktop icon** and **Reset Preferences**, and then click **Next** to continue (see Figure 1-4). Then select your icon and your preference options.

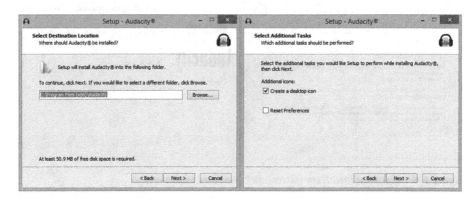

Figure 1-4. *Accept default installation options, and click Next*

Once you have specified your setup configurations, click the **Install** button (seen in the left screen in Figure 1-5). Audacity proceeds to install the software, displaying a green progress bar (shown in the right screen in Figure 1-5).

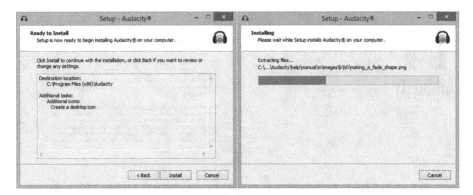

Figure 1-5. *Click the Install button to begin the installation*

After the installation process is complete, you get another **Information** dialog (see the left screen in Figure 1-6). Click the **Next** button and select the **Launch Audacity** check box. To finish the installation and launch Audacity, click the **Finish** button.

Figure 1-6. *After your install completes, click Next ånd Finish*

Be sure to create a shortcut icon for your Quick Launch taskbar in your operating system (OS), so that you can launch Audacity with just a single mouse-click.

Audio File Formats: Installing FFMPEG and LAME

If you click the **Download** tab on the Audacity homepage (see Figure 1-7), you'll see a **Plug-Ins and Libraries** link on the left, where you'll find additional plug-ins and sound libraries.

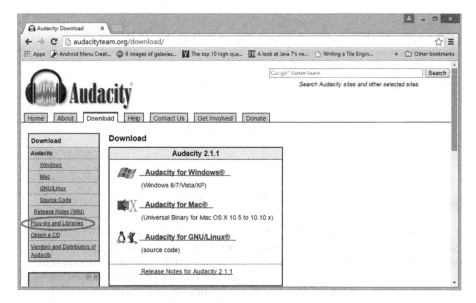

Figure 1-7. *Click the Download tab to find Plug-Ins and Libraries*

You also need to get the **LAME** and **FFMPEG** libraries, which are located on the lame.buanzo.org web site (see Figure 1-8). Click the link for Windows or for Mac, depending on what OS you are using. Linux users have libraries for LAME and FFMPEG already installed, as part of the Linux OS.

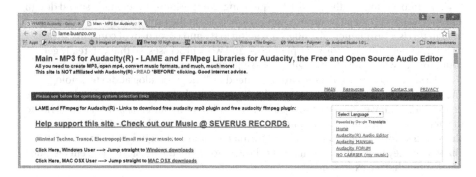

Figure 1-8. *Click the operating system link for Windows or Mac*

Since I am on Windows 8.1, I found the LAME 3.99.3 for Windows EXE file, downloaded it, and installed it onto my computer, where Audacity will find it each time it starts up.

I also downloaded and installed the FFMPEG 2.2.2 EXE file so that I will be able to import or export MPEG and other formats (see Figure 1-9).

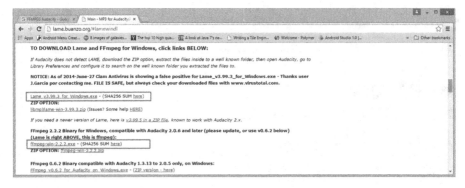

Figure 1-9. *Download LAME 3.99.3 and FFMPEG 2.2.2 libraries*

Installing these libraries is easy and requires no option specifications or shortcut icons. When you launch the Audacity software after these libraries are installed, you are able to read and write all the audio file formats covered in this book; they are supported in Android, HTML5, iOS, Java, JavaFX, Blackberry, Linux, Mac OS, and Windows.

Now let's take a look at the foundation for all audio—a sound wave, which can be generated using both analog and digital audio technology. After all, this is Chapter 1, so you should get something under your belt besides installing an impressive open source digital audio editor and a special effects software application.

A Foundation for Audio: The Sound Wave

Digital audio editing, synthesis, MIDI sequencing, composition, sweetening, sound design, and special effects can all be quite complex, especially at the professional level. Even though this is a "fundamentals" title, I am going to try and cover a lot of concepts, history, techniques, terminology, formats, platforms, and work processes, so that you really get your money's worth out of this digital audio editing fundamentals (and more) book.

Part of the complexity comes from the need to "bridge" analog audio technology and digital audio technology together. This is necessary because modern-day devices use digital audio, but we still have analog audio in our lives—in our cars, home stereos, home theaters, movie theaters, at live concerts, sports stadiums, broadcast radio, live theater, clubs, and so forth. Therefore, I cover both analog audio and digital audio in this first chapter, as they both ultimately use sound waves to create the music, dialog, effects, and other audio that we experience.

Analog Audio: Sound Waves Formed Out of Air

Analog audio is generated by using speaker cones of different sizes, which are manufactured using resilient membranes made out of one space-age material or another. Many of us have these speakers in our homes. I have 15-inch speakers right here on my desk. Larger 18- and 24-inch speakers are common in public venues, such as stadiums, theaters, and concert halls. These speakers generate sound waves by vibrating—or more accurately, pulsing—the sound waves into existence. Our ears receive these analog audio waves in exactly the opposite fashion, by catching or receiving those pulses of air, or vibrations, with different wavelengths, and then turning them back into "data" that our brain can process. This is how we "hear" the sound waves. Our brains then interpret the different audio sound wave frequencies as notes, tones, speech, sounds of nature, music, or sound effects.

A sound wave generates a different tone depending on the **frequency** of the sound wave, or the **width** (horizontal size) of the wave. Wide, long, or infrequent wave cycles produce a lower (bass) tone; whereas narrow, short, or frequent wavelengths produce a higher treble tone. Figure 1-10 visualizes this using a sine wave.

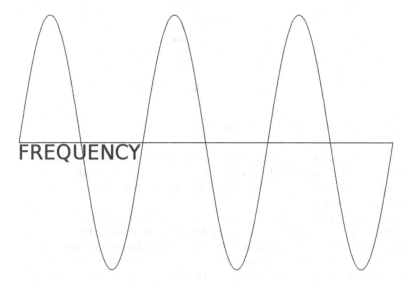

Figure 1-10. *Frequency is the width of one full wave cycle*

It is interesting to note that different frequencies of light produce different colors; so there is a very close correlation between analog sound (audio) and analog light (color). Both are "bridged" from analog to digital, and the same principles therefore carry through to digital production techniques, work processes, and principles. I point out these similarities throughout the book, in case you are interested in digital imagery compositing. In fact, I also have a *Digital Image Compositing Fundamentals* (Apress, 2015) title, which goes into these areas.

The volume of the sound wave is predicated upon the **amplitude** of that sound wave, or the **height** (vertical size) of the wave. Thus, the frequency of sound waves equates to how closely together the waves are spaced along the x axis, if you look at this in two dimensions, and the amplitude equates to how tall the waves are as measured along the y axis. This is shown in Figure 1-11 using a basic sine audio waveform.

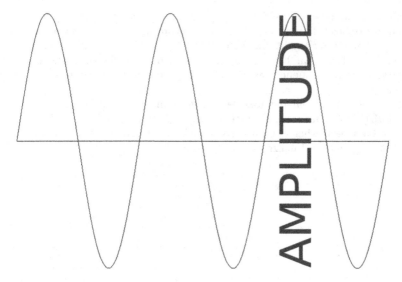

Figure 1-11. *Amplitude is the height of the sound wave*

A "baseline" sound wave type is called a **sine wave**. This type of sound wave is usually synthesized and it produces a clean, simple tone. You learned about these sine waves in your high school trigonometry class, when you learned about sine, cosine, and tangent mathematical functions.

Sound waves can be uniquely shaped, which allows them to mimic different sound effects. Those of you who are familiar with synthesizer keyboards are aware that there are many other shapes of sound waves that are used in sound design, including a **saw wave**, which looks like the edge of a saw—hence its name, or a **pulse wave**, which is shaped using right angles, resulting in immediate on-and-off sounds that translate into pulses.

Even **randomized waveforms**, such as **noise**, can be used in sound design to obtain an edgy sound result. As you will learn when we get into data footprint optimization, the more "chaos," or noise, that is present in sound waves, the harder it is to compress in the compression algorithm (codec). This results in a significantly larger digital audio data footprint for that particular sound wave. Thus, cleaner sound waves compress better than dirtier (noisier) sound waves.

Digital Audio: Sound Waves Formed Out of Bytes

The way that analog audio is "bridged" over into the digital domain is by a process called "sampling," which I cover in Chapter 3, as it is a very important topic for digital audio editing. This sound wave sampling process is one of the core tools of sound design and music synthesis, and it is named as such because you take "samples" of the analog sound wave to create a digital replica of that sound wave.

The audio wave sample has data sampled in a Y dimension, called the sample's **resolution**, and the number of samples taken in the X dimension is called the **sampling frequency**. This data sample can later be used by the digital device (smartphone, PC, tablet, e-reader, smartwatch, iTV) audio playback hardware to re-create that analog waveform and then send it back out of the speaker, or out of your headphones jack and into your headphones.

I'll cover how sampling is done and the various industry terms used, as well as the standard sample resolutions and standard sampling frequencies used in the industry.

These audio samples are used in MIDI synthesis keyboards, commonly called "samplers," as well as in sound design software such as Cakewalk SONAR, Ableton Live, or Propellerhead Reason.

Summary

In this chapter, I made sure that you had a digital audio editing software package installed and ready to master. I also covered the foundational element of both analog and digital audio, the sound wave.

You learned about sound wave frequency, or width, and amplitude, or height, and the different types of sound waves that are used in MIDI synthesizers.

Next, you looked at the concept of sampling, or taking data samples of a sound wave to convert it from an analog waveform into digital audio data.

In the next chapter, you look at the history of digital audio and the concept of MIDI sequencing.

CHAPTER 2

The History of Digital Audio: MIDI and Synthesis

Now that you've learned about the fundamental sound wave and installed a powerful open source digital audio editing software package, it's time to take a look at the history of digital audio and some of the ways that analog audio bridged over to digital audio using technologies like MIDI, synthesizers, and samplers. These impressive products and technologies are widely used today. They coalesce to create digital audio workstations, or DAWs, which provide a powerful fusion of sound design, audio editing, and music composition capabilities.

I'll show you another open source digital audio software package called Rosegarden, which focuses less on digital audio and more on MIDI, music composition, and music scoring, which is the process of turning notes into professional staff notation.

Downloading and Installing Rosegarden

If you are interested in other areas of digital audio besides editing, such as music composition, I cover those in this chapter as well, so that you get the full picture of the fusion of MIDI, synthesis, and sampling that is possible with today's digital audio content production software packages.

For some reason, the Linux operating system currently features the most impressive DAW software packages, including QTractor and Rosegarden. Fortunately, Rosegarden is being ported to Windows, too, so I will expose you to it in this chapter. I also cover other digital audio production tools and show you how they can be fused with audio sampling to create a scenario where you seamlessly use all of these technologies to achieve massive audio-content production power. This does not come without a measure of complexity, which is why I am exposing you to the fundamentals.

Rosegarden.com: Get Your Rosegarden Software

If you want to be a songwriter as well as a digital audio engineer, you can download Rosegarden at http://rosegardenmusic.com. Not only is Rosegarden a MIDI sequencer, but it also includes music notation, also known as **scoring**. This means that you don't

Electronic supplementary material The online version of this chapter (doi:10.1007/978-1-4842-1648-4_2) contains supplementary material, which is available to authorized users.

W. Jackson, *Digital Audio Editing Fundamentals*, DOI 10.1007/978-1-4842-1648-4_2

have to know how to write notes and clefs on staffs to publish your music! To download Rosegarden 15.10, which is the current stable version, click the **Get Rosegarden** link. If you need the Windows version, go to the Xyglo web site at **http://xyglo.com/ rosegarden-for-windows/** (see Figure 2-1), as I did, and download version 15.10.

Figure 2-1. *Go to the xyglo.com/rosegarden-for-windows/ web page*

Download the **rosegarden-win32-alpha-4.exe** installer file if you are using Windows (otherwise, download the Linux version), and then double-click it to start the installation process. Currently, there is no Mac OS X version of this software. (But contact Apple and ask for it—maybe they will listen to your request for Mac support!)

Rosegarden for Windows is a 32-bit version; if you want to run the 64-bit Rosegarden, then use Linux. Once the installation starts, read the licensing agreement, and then click the **I Agree** button.

Next, select the check boxes for the components that you wish to install. I selected **Rosegarden ➤ Fonts ➤ Start Menu Shortcuts**. Click the **Next** button and select your destination folder (I used the default `C:\Program Files (x86)\Xyglo\Rosegarden\`). Finally, click the **Install** button. You are then shown an installation progress bar and a **Show Details** button.

Once you launch Rosegarden the first time, you see a **Welcome!** dialog (see Figure 2-2), which provides suggestions on plug-ins, audio servers, synthesizer software (MIDI generates no sound; it is performance-only, which you will see later in this chapter), tutorials, web sites, and documentation.

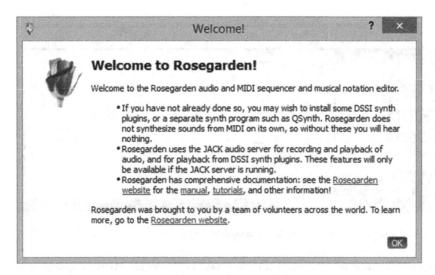

Figure 2-2. Rosegarden Welcome! dialog containing important information

Once you click the **OK** button in the Welcome! dialog, you see an empty Rosegarden project, as shown in Figure 2-3.

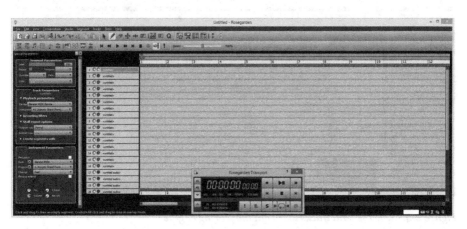

Figure 2-3. Rosegarden software on start-up, with empty project

Let's look at some MIDI data and the Rosegarden user interface by opening the open source **fidelio.mid** file. As you can see in Figure 2-4, there is a transport, which you can position anywhere on your screen, and MIDI tracks in the primary editing view of the software. On the left, there is a **control panel** that contains **parameters** for segment, track, and instrument selections. Along the top, there are icons that allow access to the Rosegarden recording, editing, and scoring features.

Figure 2-4. Open source fidelio.mid MIDI sample data file

Let's take a look at how Rosegarden 14 automatically scores any **MIDI composition data** into **musical score publishing**. Select five of the performance tracks by holding down the **SHIFT** key and clicking the five tracks that are shown on the right side of Figure 2-5, invoking Rosegarden's **multi-select** feature.

Figure 2-5. Select several tracks to try out the scoring engine

Click the Notation (Note) icon (the third option in the second icon bar on the left side of the screen). This opens the Notation window shown in Figure 2-6, where you can see that Rosegarden can turn your MIDI performances (keyboard keys) into professional staff notation containing notes and timing. Amazing software!

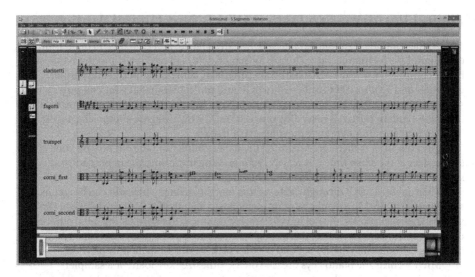

Figure 2-6. *Showing music notation features of Rosegarden 14.02*

Now that I have shown you Rosegarden and MIDI data, and what it can become, let's get into MIDI and the history of audio.

The Digital Audio Player Piano: MIDI Data

Digital audio editing, synthesis, MIDI sequencing, composition, sweetening, sound design, and special effects can all be quite complex, especially at the professional level. Even though this is a "fundamentals" book, I am going to try to cover a lot of concepts, history, techniques, terminology, software, formats, content delivery platforms, and work processes, so that you really get your money's worth.

MIDI Data: Your Musical Instrument Data Interface

MIDI stands for **Musical Instrument Data Interface**. It was one of the very first ways that anyone could work with audio using a personal computer—as long as you had a 5-pin MIDI port connected to a MIDI interface, and drivers that allowed your operating system to see and talk to the MIDI interface. The origins of MIDI date all the way back to the 1980s, so MIDI has been "in play" (no pun intended) for more than 30 years. MIDI holds an important role in the evolution of digital audio, and is a key component of music synthesis and sound design.

The first computer to feature integrated MIDI ports and MIDI interface hardware was Atari's ST1040. This MIDI computer allowed me to plug my keyboard synthesizer (at the time, it was a Yamaha DX7) into the MIDI ports. MIDI allowed me to play and digitally record my **performance data** using a computer, which used a **MIDI data format**, along with audio software known as a **MIDI sequencer**, which sequenced playback data using **tracks**, allowing me to build up my musical composition over time.

15

Digital Performance Data: MIDI Is Not Digital Audio

A MIDI file contains no audio data; that is, the MIDI file format contains no digital audio, only **digital performance data**. This performance data is played back into the synthesizer by the computer, using the MIDI hardware (interface, cables, and ports) that connects the computer and synthesizer together with an **in** and **out** cable, so that your computer and synthesizers can talk to each other. As the computer is playing back your existing track using the synth **in port**, it is recording the next track, which you are composing as you listen to the computer play your previous MIDI tracks.

The computer is therefore recording the data coming from the out port on your synthesizer at the same time it is playing your existing tracks into the in port on your synthesizer. Fortunately, computers are able to process MIDI data rapidly!

There is also a MIDI **through cable**, so that more than one synthesizer can be connected simultaneously. My MIDI synthesis setup includes the Yamaha TX-802, which is eight DX-7 synths in one rack mount, the Roland D-50 rack mount, and the Korg Z1. My setup only needs one keyboard synthesizer due to this through port, because performance data that I played on a Korg Z1 routes into the TX-802 and D-50 for rack-mount synth module playback.

MIDI records the piano keys pressed on a synthesizer keyboard or a sampler keyboard. It also records the keypress duration, the amount of pressure the key was pressed with (the **aftertouch**), and similar playback performance nuances.

It is important to note a third type of keyboard, called a **controller**, which is used only to generate MIDI performance data. It looks like a synthesizer or sampler keyboard, but it requires a rack-mount synthesizer or sampler, or digital audio software, to trigger samples or synthesize the sound waves that the MIDI performance data would trigger.

Audio Synthesis: Synthesizers Create Sound Waves

MIDI performance is silent. As you have seen with Rosegarden, it records your performance data, while the digital audio waveforms created by that performance are actually made with your keyboard synthesizer. Your synthesizer, or "synth," generates artificial or "synthesized" audio tones using the MIDI performance data to specify how to create your digital audio (synthesized) sound waves. A **sampling keyboard** plays back a digital audio sample (pre-recorded waveform) based on the MIDI performance data. It provides an even more aural-realistic (like photo-realistic imagery) performance, because each note on the instrument is sampled, or recorded, whether it is a piano, guitar, bass, fiddle, banjo, horn, flute, oboe, or drums.

When MIDI files are played back through the synthesizer, or through a sampler, it replicates the exact performance of the performer or the composer; even though that person is no longer playing the performance track, the computer is playing it back.

Let's discuss the way MIDI data is used in MIDI sequencer software. You play an instrument track, record the instrument performance for your music composition using MIDI data, and the MIDI sequencer then plays the performance while you play a second instrument track—alongside the first instrument's performance track.

While the computer is handling the MIDI performance data (recording and playback), the controller keyboard is handling the performance data generation and the rack-mount synthesizer or sampler is processing the performance playback MIDI data, which it is receiving from the MIDI sequencer software.

MIDI enables songwriters to assemble complex musical compositions and to refine them into any number of arrangements using only a personal computer, a synthesizer, a sampler, or a digital audio production software package. Composing or arranging in your home on a workstation costs less money than hiring a recording studio full of studio musicians! This is why I had you download and install Rosegarden—so that you can play around with MIDI, which makes the concept easier to understand.

MIDI Platform Support: Android, HTML5, and Java

All the open source platforms support MIDI files, including Android, HTML5, Java, and JavaFX. I expect closed platforms such as iOS and Windows to also support MIDI performance data playback. It is important to note, however, that **MIDI playback hardware**, such as a synthesizer or a sample library, must be in place for MIDI playback to succeed.

MIDI playback is also possible when a **MIDI playback software** capability that mimics MIDI playback hardware (audio synthesis or sampler) is installed. For this reason, MIDI is best utilized in an audio production and music composition scenario; although not so much in a content delivery scenario.

Data footprint optimization can be significant when using MIDI. These data-heavy waveforms can be stored on the "client side" and "rendered" by extremely data-compact MIDI performance data as needed by your musical composition. This is significant because the same note needs to be recorded only once (see Chapter 3), but can be used in a composition a million times by using the same data in memory. The more complex programming and optimization principles are covered at the end of this book.

Android OS supports the playback of MIDI files, but it does not implement a MIDI class for their creation. I hope that this changes in the future, but as it sits right now, it is not an easy job to code MIDI sequencers in Android Studio; however, this is being discussed in çoding forums.

JavaFX also supports the playback of MIDI file formats, as does HTML5, so devices such as iTVs, tablets, e-readers, smartphones, and smartwatches support MIDI if you need to utilize it for your multimedia production projects.

Summary

In this chapter, I made sure that you had a MIDI sequencing and scoring software package installed and ready to master, just in case you want to be a music composer and an arranger, in addition to being a digital audio editor and engineer. You looked at the history of bridging analog audio with digital audio, and I discussed MIDI, MIDI sequencers, synthesizer keyboards, MIDI controllers, and sampler keyboards.

You learned about how MIDI works using only performance data, how controllers can generate that data, and how synthesizers or samplers can generate sound waves (covered in Chapter 1) using this MIDI performance data.

In the next chapter, you look at the concept of sampling, or taking data samples of the sound wave to convert it from analog waveforms into a digital audio data format.

CHAPTER 3

The Reproduction of Digital Audio: Data Sampling

Now that you know the general history of digital audio, it is time to get into digital audio sampling (essentially the same as digital audio recording), which needs to be done before any digital audio editing can be done. This chapter covers the concepts behind "digitizing" analog audio—or turning it into digital audio—by defining which **sampling frequency** is utilized during the digitization process and which **sample resolution** is used to store individual samples of analog audio waveforms as digital audio data.

In addition to digital audio sampling concepts, such as sampling frequency and sample resolution, you also look at standard sampling frequencies and sample resolutions, which are used in the digital audio industry, and how to sample, or record, digital audio by using Audacity 2.1.1 for Windows.

Data Sampling: Resolution and Frequency

In this chapter, I cover the process of **digital audio data sampling**. You will see how the transition can be made between analog audio and digital audio using the process of sampling, which you are already familiar with if you do sound design and music synthesis.

Sampling is even discussed in the news, as recording artists are sometimes sued for taking little "riffs" or "snippets" of another artist's song and sampling it in their songs. For this reason, be very careful with what you are sampling; make sure that it is an original analog audio waveform or that you have permission to use it! I want to make sure that you have a firm understanding of the digital audio new media assets that you will eventually create, optimize, and "render" via open source APIs, such as Java and JavaFX, or the Android Studio digital audio playback classes, SoundPool and MediaPlayer.

Sampling Digital Audio: Taking a Data Sample

The process of turning analog audio (sound waves) into digital audio data is called **sampling**. If you work in the music industry, you have probably heard about a type of keyboard (or rack-mount equipment) called a "sampler." Specifically, sampling is the

Electronic supplementary material The online version of this chapter (doi:10.1007/978-1-4842-1648-4_3) contains supplementary material, which is available to authorized users.

process of slicing an audio wave into segments so that you can store the shape of that wave as digital audio sample data, which is later reproduced using a hardware device with digital audio support. The sample data can be stored by using a codec and digital audio file format, which is discussed in Chapter 4.

Audio data sampling turns infinitely accurate analog sound waves into discreet (finite) digital audio data; that is, into a collection of zeroes and ones, often called **binary data**.

The more zeroes and ones that are used, the more infinitely accurate the reproduction of the original analog sound wave will be. The sample accuracy determines the number of zeroes and ones that are used to reproduce an analog sound wave; these sample accuracy topics are covered next.

Data Sample Resolution: Data Bytes per Sample

Each **digital slice** of your sampled audio sound wave is called a sample because it takes a sampling of your sound wave at an exact point in time. The precision, or resolution, of each sample is determined by the amount of data that is utilized to define each wave slice height, or the **amplitude**. Just as with digital imaging, this precision is termed the **resolution**, or more accurately (no pun intended), your **digital audio waveform sample resolution**.

It is important to remember that digital audio resolution takes samples along the amplitude of your audio waveform, which takes place along the y axis of the audio sample waveform (if you are looking at the data using a 2D representation). This is shown in Figure 3-1, where the amplitude is measured by the height of the waveform; in this case, it is a simple sine wave used for visualization purposes. You may have learned about sine waves in school. Simple tones can be produced by audio oscillator hardware using sine waves, as you will see in the more advanced chapters of the book when you use the Audacity Generate menu to create waveforms algorithmically. In Chapter 5, you begin a lot of hands-on audio editing using the Audacity 2.1.1 audio production software package. For now, let's just cover the basics.

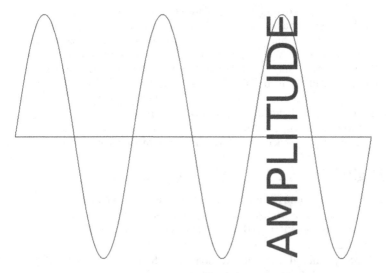

Figure 3-1. *Data resolution is specified using wave amplitude*

Digital audio sample resolutions are defined with 8-bit, 12-bit, 16-bit, 24-bit, or 32-bit data. In digital imaging and digital video, data resolution is quantified by the number of 8-bit color channels; in digital audio, the resolution is quantified by the number of bytes of data used to define each of the audio samples being taken. Audacity samples at 32-bit data resolution, because you want to start high and then optimize digital audio to one of the mainstream lower resolutions (as you'll see in Chapter 12, where digital audio data footprint optimization is discussed).

Except for the 12-bit resolution for digital audio, which is actually rarely used, the 8-bit, 16-bit, 24-bit, and 32-bit data packet resolutions match up identically between digital imagery editing and digital audio editing. The most commonly used audio data resolutions are 8 bits in low-quality sound effects or voice tracks, 16 bits in music, and 24 bits in HD audio (again, music).

As with digital images, where more color yields a better image quality, in digital audio, a higher sample resolution always yields a better sound wave reproduction.

Thus, higher sampling resolutions, or using more data to reproduce a given sound wave sample, yields a higher audio playback quality at the expense of a larger data footprint.

This is the reason why 16-bit audio, termed "CD quality" audio, sounds better than 8-bit audio; just like true color JPEG or PNG24 imagery should always look better than 8-bit GIF indexed color images. Having a 12-bit digital audio resolution is a valuable option for getting higher quality vocal tracks or sound effects without having to use 16-bit or 24-bit data, because these audio data resolutions are more appropriate for high-quality music experiences or for the audio track in a film or digital video production.

In digital audio broadcasting, there's a trend in using a 24-bit digital audio sampling resolution, known as "HD audio" in the consumer electronics industry.

HD digital audio broadcast radio and satellite radio now use a 24-bit data sampling resolution, so each audio sample, or slice of a sound wave, contains 16,777,216 (this is 24 bits in decimal) potential sample-resolution numeric accuracy.

Some of the newer iOS, Android, and Blackberry devices now support HD audio, starting with the smartphone products that are advertised as featuring HD-quality digital audio playback hardware (a 24-bit capable audio data decoding hardware chip). In order for a hardware device to play the HD audio format, you must have 24-bit audio hardware. I recommend using the 16-bit audio for the widest playback compatibility.

Data Sample Frequency: Data Samples per Second

Besides a digital audio sample resolution, you also have a digital audio **sampling frequency**. This defines the number of data samples, at any given sample resolution, which are taken during one second of sample time. In digital imagery, sampling frequency is analogous to the number of pixels that are contained in a digital image. Sampling frequency is sometimes termed a **sampling rate**. You are familiar with the term CD quality audio, which is defined as using a 16-bit sample resolution and a 44.1 kHz sampling rate. This is taking 44,100 samples, each of which contains 16 bits of sample resolution, or the potential maximum 65,536 data values, for digital audio data held in each sample.

The sampling frequency is taken along the other (x) axis of the sound wave, or waveform, than the resolution is, so that each sample can also have a resolution.

The sampling rate is the number of resolution data samples in a full second of audio data along the frequency dimension of a digital audio waveform, as illustrated in Figure 3-2.

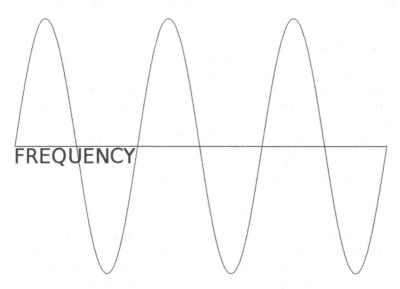

Figure 3-2. *The number of data samples are taken over the frequency*

Common audio sample rates for the digital audio industry include 8 kHz, 11.25 kHz, 22.5 kHz, 32 kHz, 44.1 kHz, 48 kHz, 96 kHz, 192k Hz, and recently, 384 kHz. As you may have noticed, I like to use the ones that are evenly divisible by a power of two (8-bit), and so I gravitate toward 8 kHz (low quality), 32 kHz (medium quality), and 48 kHz (high quality).

Lower sampling rates, such as 8 kHz or 11.25 kHz, should be optimal for sampling "voice-based" digital audio, as well as sound effects, such as game sound effects, dialog tracks, or an audio e-book narration track, for example.

Medium-quality audio sample rates, such as 22.5 kHz or 32 kHz, are more appropriate in background music loops in games and some sound effects, such as rumbling thunder, which absolutely needs to have a high dynamic range to ensure higher fidelity digital audio reproduction. The same goes for using 22.5 kHz on vocal tracks in high-quality vocals.

Higher audio sample rates, such as 44 kHz or 48 kHz, are more appropriate for music, which usually requires your highest fidelity reproduction.

Some sound effects, or even music, can get away with using lower 22.5 kHz or 32 kHz sampling rates, as long as the sampling resolution used is 16-bit quality or higher.

Ultimately, you have to use your ears as your guide during the digital audio optimization process, which you'll do in Chapter 12 after you create and edit a data sample and need to ascertain what your "aural quality-to-digital audio asset file size" trade-off is going to be.

Data Sample Mathematics: Amount of Binary Data

Let's do some math to find out the number of bits of data that might be held in one second of **raw** (uncompressed) digital audio data. This is calculated by multiplying the sample resolution by the sampling frequency. A 16-bit sample resolution contains 65,536 potential data samples, and the sampling frequency is 44,100 samples per second. Multiplying these yields 2,890,137,600 data values available to represent one second of CD quality audio.

Digital audio data codecs compress this down to an amazingly small file size. The initial raw data footprint size is the starting point for digital audio data footprint optimization. So if you can get adequate quality using a lower sample resolution and (or) a lower sampling rate, the digital audio compression algorithm (codec) is able to do a much better job of exporting a more compact data file; that is, a smaller digital audio file size.

The same trade-off you have with a digital imaging asset exists with digital audio. If you include more data, you get a high-quality result at the cost of a larger file size. Audio codecs do a great encoding job. Fortunately, digital audio has better quality-to–file size results than digital imagery.

Sample Products: Sampler Hardware and Libraries

Although this book includes the work process for creating your own digital audio data samples, you can also obtain third-party, professional digital audio data samples in a number of different formats, including sampler keyboards and rack-mount hardware, sampler software, and sample libraries, which come on CD-ROM, DVD-ROM, or EPROM chips that install in the keyboard or rack-mount sampler hardware. If you want to be a composer, this is the best option because the instrument samples are done for you, so you can focus on creating musical compositions.

The most expensive sampling hardware is keyboard samplers, because they have a MIDI controller and a sample playback hardware architecture in one completely integrated instrument. Rack-mount sampler hardware is significantly less expensive, because it only has the sampler playback hardware and few moving parts other than some knobs, dials, sliders, and LCD readouts.

The next step down in expense is sample playback software. You need a MIDI controller to use it. This is the next most expensive option because it uses the computer processor as sample processing hardware to play the samples. With this solution, sample data comes on a CD-ROM or DVD-ROM, and is loaded onto the hard disk and played back by the sampler software using a MIDI controller after the instrument samples are loaded into the system memory.

Recording Digital Audio: Using Audacity

Since this is the third chapter, let's start the process of using Audacity to record a data sample and to see how Audacity works. As you can see in Figure 3-3, Audacity's audio recording levels are located at the top center of the screen, exactly where they should be. Click **Click to Start Monitoring** to learn the ambient sound levels that your microphone is recording in your room. Audio levels show you the amplitude of the sound waves that you are recording.

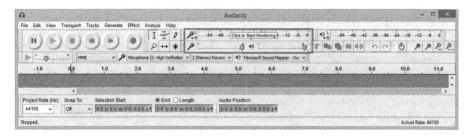

Figure 3-3. *Launch Audacity and click Click to Start Monitoring*

You can see these levels (they animate, based on ambient noise) in Figure 3-4. I left Audacity at the default settings, because you will remove your ambient background noise in Chapter 6, which covers the Audacity noise removal algorithm and work process.

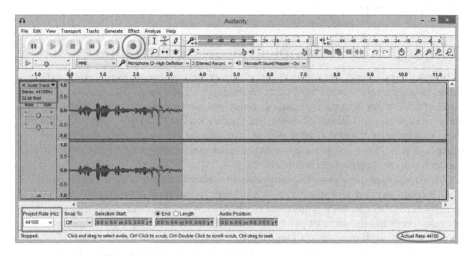

Figure 3-4. *Use the record button to record your voice at 44.1 kHz*

To the left of the digital audio level meters you see the **audio transport controls**. These include your standard **play** and **pause** buttons, as well as **stop** and **record** buttons. I've circled the record button, which you click and then say "digital audio editing fundamentals," into your desktop microphone. I used a $9 Logitech stand microphone from Walmart on my workstation.

When you are finished recording, click the **stop** button to end the recording process. You see the sound waves shown in Figure 3-4 (or something similar) in the middle of the Audacity window.

As you can see in the bottom-right corner of Figure 3-4, Audacity shows you the actual sampling rate (sampling frequency) used in this waveform data (this is shown in the middle of the editing window). You can set the actual sampling rate before recording using the **Project Rate (Hz)** drop-down menu at the bottom-left corner. The sample rate and the sample resolution are shown on the left side of Figure 3-4; just as I said, the default Audacity sample settings are 32-bit resolution with a CD-quality 44.1 kHz sample frequency.

Now that you have the sample data that you'll be refining over the next few chapters, let's save your project, which you always want to do after creating any sample. This is done using the Audacity **File ➤ Save Project** menu sequence, as shown in Figure 3-5.

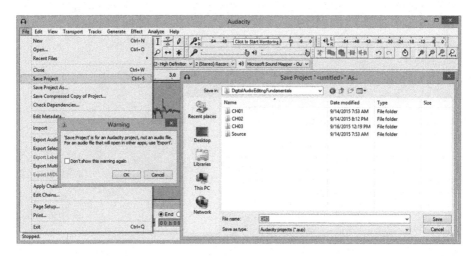

Figure 3-5. *Save you Audacity project using File ➤ Save Project*

The first thing that you see is a **Warning** dialog that informs you that an AUP file format is not an audio (playback) file format, but instead an **AU**dacity **P**roject data file format. This is shown on the left in Figure 3-5. Click the **OK** button, enter a **File name** for your Audacity project, and then click the **Save** button. I saved this sample as **CH3.AUP** in case you want to use it during Chapters 5–8.

Summary

In this chapter, you learned about digital audio data sampling concepts, techniques, and principles, as well as how to calculate sample data and how to record your own data samples using Audacity 2.1.1. You also learned about samplers and sample resolution along the y axis and sampling frequency along the x axis.

In the next chapter, you learn about **digital audio data formats** and **digital audio data transmission** principles.

CHAPTER 4

The Transmission of Digital Audio: Data Formats

Now that you understand the fundamental concepts, terms, and principles behind analog audio and how it is digitized into digital audio, it is time to explore how digital audio is compressed and stored using popular open source digital audio file formats.

You'll learn about advanced digital audio concepts, such as compression, codecs, bit rates, streaming audio, captive digital audio, and HD audio. Finally, you'll look at a number of powerful digital audio formats that are supported by open source content development platforms, such as HTML5, Java, JavaFX, and Android Studio. You can use any of the digital audio formats to deliver digital audio content for podcasts, music publishing, web site design, audio broadcasts, or multimedia applications.

Audio Compression and Data Formats

Once you sample your audio, you compress it into a digital audio file format for streaming over the Web or for captive audio file playback within an application. In this chapter, you'll look at encoding audio using bit rates, and learn about streaming and the new 24-bit HD audio standard, which is now utilized in broadcast and satellite radio. I'll also cover audio codecs and the audio file formats that they support across open platforms, such as HTML5, Java, and Android. (I cover digital audio data footprint optimization in Chapter 12, after you learn more about Audacity and digital audio editing.)

I want to make sure that you have a deep understanding of these digital audio new media assets so that you can eventually "render" them inside of your target application and attain a professional product that offers an impeccable end-user experience.

Digital Audio Codecs: Bit Rates, Streaming, and HD

Digital audio assets are compressed using something called a **codec**, which stands for "**co**de **dec**ode." The codec is an **algorithm** that applies **data compression** to digital audio samples and determines which playback rate, called a **bit rate**, it will use, as well as if it will support **streaming** or playback during network data transfer. First, let's take a look at how you use digital audio assets in your applications: Do you store audio inside an

© Wallace Jackson 2015
W. Jackson, *Digital Audio Editing Fundamentals*, DOI 10.1007/978-1-4842-1648-4_4

application or do you stream it from remote servers over the Internet? After that, you'll consider the audio playback rate or data-streaming bit rate that you'll want to use. Finally, you'll learn about HD audio and see if it's appropriate for your digital audio applications. Only then will you be ready to look at the different audio file formats, which are actually codecs!

Digital Audio Transmission: Streaming Audio or Captive Audio?

Just as with digital video, which you view on the Internet every day, digital audio assets can either be **captive**, or contained within an application (for example, in an Android APK file), or they can be **streamed** using a remote data server. Similar to digital video, the upside to streaming digital audio data is that it can reduce the data footprint (size) of your application's files. The downside is reliability.

Streaming audio saves the data footprint, because you don't have to include all that data-heavy new media digital audio in your app file. Thus, if you are planning on coding a Jukebox application, you want to consider streaming digital audio data, as you would not want to pack your song library into your app's file because it would be 10 gigabytes (in a large library).

Otherwise, for application audio, such as user interface feedback sounds, game play audio, and so forth, try to optimize your digital audio data so that you can include it inside your app file as a captive asset. In this way, it is available to your application users when needed.

As you know, I'll go over optimization in Chapter 12, after digital audio editing has been covered. The reason that I want to cover this topic toward the end of the book is that the last step in the asset creation process is exporting your digital audio data using one of the formats discussed in the next section.

The downside to streaming digital audio is that if your user's connection (or your audio server) goes down, your audio file won't be present for your end users to play and listen to! The reliability and availability of a digital audio data stream is a key factor to consider on the other side of the streaming audio vs. captive digital audio decision.

Streaming Digital Audio Data: Setting Your Bit Rates Optimally

One of the primary concepts in streaming your digital audio is the bit rate of that digital audio data. Again, this is very similar to digital video, which also uses the concept of bit rates to determine the size of the data pipe that the audio data streams through. The digital audio bit rate is defined during digital audio file compression by the settings that you give to the codec.

Digital audio files that need to support a lower bit rate to accommodate slower bandwidth networks have more compression applied to the digital audio data. This results in a lower audio-quality level. However, lower playback quality isn't as noticeable in digital audio as it is in digital video.

Low bit-rate digital audio can always play back smoothly across a greater number of hardware devices. This is because if there are fewer bytes of audio data to transfer over any given data network, then there are fewer digital audio data bytes to be processed by the CPU inside that hardware device.

As a processor gets faster, it can process more bytes per second. As a data bandwidth connection gets faster, it can more comfortably send or receive more bytes per second.

Therefore, it is important to remember that you are not only optimizing your audio file size for network transfers, but you are also optimizing your digital audio assets for the amount of system memory that asset requires, as well as the amount of processing cycles that the CPU uses to process the digital audio asset sample data.

High-Definition HD Digital Audio: 24-Bit 48 kHz Sampling Data

As I mentioned in Chapter 3, the industry baseline for superior standard definition (SD) audio quality is known as CD quality audio, which is defined as a 16-bit data sample resolution and the 44.1 kHz data sampling frequency. It was used to produce audio CD products way back in the 20th century and it is still used as a minimum digital audio quality standard.

There is also a more recent HD audio standard that uses a 24-bit data sample at a 48 kHz or a 96 kHz sample frequency. It is used today in HD radio and HD satellites, as well as in HD audio–compatible Android devices, such as the new Droid X HD "high-fidelity" Android smartphones. These provide the user with an extremely high-fidelity digital audio experience. HD audio is supported by several of the open source codecs.

Digital Audio Storage and Playback: File Formats

There are considerably more digital audio codecs supported in the open platforms (HTML5, Java, or Android) than digital imaging codecs, as there are only four image codecs: PNG, JPEG, GIF, and WebP. Android Studio audio support, for instance, includes MP3 (MPEG-3) files, WAV or AIFF (PCM) files, MP4 or M4A (MPEG4) files, OGG files, FLAC files, and MID, MXMF, and XMF MIDI files, which as you know from Chapter 2 are not really digital audio data. Let's cover all the digital audio formats that support sampled (digitized waveform) data.

MIDI: Musical Instrument Data Interface's MID, XMF, and MXMF

Since MIDI was covered in Chapter 2, I will just go over the different file formats supported in open platforms, such as HTML5 (browsers and operating systems), Java (using JavaFX), and Android Studio. There are several MIDI file formats, including MID, XMF, and MXMF MIDI formats. They are exceptionally compact because there is zero waveform data; there is only performance data, such as note on, note off, aftertouch, and so on. You opened and scored a MIDI file named fidelio.mid using Rosegarden in Chapter 2!

MPEG-3: The Popular MP3 Digital Audio Player Data Format

The most popular digital audio format in history is the **MP3** digital audio file format, which is short for MPEG-3. Most of you are familiar with the MP3 digital audio files found on music download web sites such as Napster. Most of us collected songs in this format to use on popular MP3 players or in CD-ROM music collections. The reason this MP3 digital audio file format is popular is because it has a relatively good **compression-to-quality ratio**, and because the codec needed to play MP3 audio files is found everywhere, including Android, iOS, Blackberry, Windows, Java, JavaFX, and HTML5.

MP3 is an acceptable format to use in your web site or application as long as you can get the highest quality level possible out of it by using the optimal encoding work process (again, this will be covered in Chapter 12).

Because of software patents, Audacity 2 can't include MP3 encoding software or distribute any MP3 software from its own web site, which is why I showed you how to download and install the free LAME and FFMPEG encoders for Audacity.

It's important to note that the MP3 codec outputs a **lossy** compression audio file format. Lossy compression is where some of the audio data, and thus quality, is discarded during a data compression process; it cannot be recovered. This is similar to the JPEG compression algorithm for digital images, which can cause visual artifacts (purple, green, or yellow pixel smudges).

Open platforms do support the open source **lossless** audio codec called FLAC, which stands for **Free Lossless Audio Codec**. Support for FLAC is now as widespread as MP3, due to the free nature of the software decoder.

FLAC: The 24-Bit HD Audio Capable Free Lossless Audio Codec

FLAC uses a fast algorithm, so the decoder is highly optimized for speed. FLAC supports 24-bit audio, and there are no patent concerns for using it. It is a great audio codec to use in Android or HTML5 if you need high-quality audio with a reasonable data footprint (file size). FLAC supports a range of sample resolutions, from 4-bit data per sample, up to 32-bit data sampling. It also supports a wide range of sample frequencies, from 1 Hz to 65,535 Hz (or 65 kHz), using 1 Hz increments; it is extremely flexible. From an audio playback hardware standpoint, I suggest using a 16-bit sample resolution and either a 44.1 kHz or a 48 kHz sample frequency, unless you're targeting HD audio, in which case you should use 24-bit with 48 kHz for HD audio.

FLAC is supported in Android 3.1 and Java. Therefore, if your end users are using current Android devices, you should be able to safely utilize the FLAC codec. It is possible to use completely lossless new media assets in Android application development by using PNG8, PNG24, PNG32, and FLAC, as long as your application is targeting Android 3.1 or later hardware devices. Next, let's take a look at another impressive open source codec.

Ogg Vorbis: A Lossy High-Performance Open Source Codec

Another open source digital audio codec supported by Android is the **Ogg Vorbis** format. This lossy audio codec is brought to you by the Xiph.Org Foundation. The Vorbis codec data is usually held inside an **OGG** audio data file extension, and thus, Vorbis is commonly called the Ogg Vorbis digital audio data format.

Ogg Vorbis supports sampling rates from 8 kHz to 192 kHz, and supports 255 discrete channels of digital audio. As you now know, this represents 8-bits worth of audio channels. Ogg Vorbis is supported across all Android versions or API-level releases.

Vorbis is quickly approaching the quality of MPEG HE-AAC and Windows Media Audio (WMA) Professional, and it is superior in quality to MP3, AAC-LC, and WMA. It's a lossy format, so the FLAC codec still has superior reproduction quality over Ogg Vorbis, as FLAC contains all the original digital audio sample data. Ogg Vorbis audio and Ogg Theora video are supported in HTML5.

MPEG-4: Advanced Audio Coding AAC-LC, AAC-ELD, or HE-AAC

Android, with a market share in the 90% range across all hardware devices, supports all the MPEG-4 AAC (Advanced Audio Coding) codecs, including **AAC-LC, HE-AAC,** and **AAC-ELD.** Java, which is the development and publishing platform that is nearing 90% market share among developers, also supports these codecs. AAC audio data samples are contained using MPEG-4 file "containers" (.3gp, .mp4, or .m4a file extensions). AAC-LC and HE-AAC can be decoded with all versions of Android. The AAC-ELD is only supported after Android OS 4.1. ELD stands for **Enhanced Low Delay**; this codec is intended for use in real-time, two-way communications applications, such as a digital walkie-talkies, or Dick Tracy–style smartwatch apps.

The simplest AAC codec is the AAC-LC (Low Complexity) codec, which is the most widely used. This is sufficient for most digital audio encoding applications. AAC-LC yields a higher quality result at a lower data footprint than the MP3 codec.

The most complicated AAC codec, HE-AAC (High Efficiency) codec, supports sampling rates from 8 kHz to 48 kHz, and both stereo and Dolby 5.1 channel encoding. Android decodes both V1 and V2 levels of HE-AAC. Android can also **encode** audio using the HE-AAC-V1 codec in Android devices later than version 4.1.

Because of software patents, Audacity doesn't include an MPEG-4 encoder. Be sure to download and install the free FFMPEG 2.2.2 encoder for Audacity, from http://lame. buanzo.org before you start Chapter 5, where you'll use Audacity 2.1.1. You should have done this in Chapter 1, so just make sure that you have the libraries installed to maximize Audacity's features!

AMR: The MPEG-4 Adaptive Multi-Rate Audio Codecs for Voice

For encoding speech, which usually features a different type of sound wave than music does, there are also two other **AMR** (Adaptive Multi-Rate) audio codecs, which are extremely efficient for encoding things like speech or "short-burst" sound effects.

There is an **AMR-WB** (Adaptive Multi-Rate Wideband) codec in Android that supports nine discrete settings, from a 6.6 kbps bit rate up to 23.85 kbps, sampled at 16 kHz. This is a pretty high sampling rate where voice is concerned! This is the codec to use on Narrator tracks, if you're creating interactive e-book Android Studio applications, for example.

There's also an **AMR-NB** (Adaptive Multi-Rate Narrowband) codec in Android that supports eight discrete settings, from 4.75 kbps to 12.2 kbps audio bit rates sampled at 8 kHz. This is an adequate sample rate if the data going into the codec is high quality or if resulting audio samples do not require high quality due to the noisy nature of the content (for example, a bomb blast).

Pulse-Code Modulation: Windows WAV or Mac AIFF PCM Codecs

Finally, almost all operating systems, including Windows, Mac OS, and Linux-based ones, such as Android, Tizen, Ubuntu, openSUSE, Blackberry, Firefox OS, Opera OS, and Chrome OS, support the **PCM** (pulse-code modulation) codecs, commonly known as the Windows WAVE (WAV) audio format or the Apple AIFF (Audio Interchange File Format). Most of you are familiar with this lossless digital audio format from one of these two popular operating systems. It is lossless because there is zero compression applied. PCM audio is commonly used for CD-ROM content, as well as telephony applications. This is because PCM Wave audio is an uncompressed digital audio format. It has no CPU-intensive compression algorithms applied to the data stream, and thus decoding (CPU overhead) is not an issue for telephony equipment or for CD players.

For this reason, when we start compressing digital audio assets into various file formats in Chapter 12, which covers digital audio data footprint optimization, you will use PCM as the "baseline" file format.

You probably won't put PCM into Kindle (MOBI), Java (JAR), or Android (APK) distributable files, however, because there are other formats, such as FLAC and MPEG-4 AAC, which give you the same quality, and do it using an order of magnitude less data.

Ultimately, the only way to find out which audio formats supported by Android have the best digital audio result for any given audio data is to actually encode digital audio in all the primary codecs that you know are well supported and efficient. I show you how this is accomplished in Chapter 12.

Summary

In this chapter, you looked at the digital audio data encoding concepts, principles, and file formats used to compress and decompress digital audio assets, as well as to publish and distribute to end users. You also learned how sample resolution, sample frequency, bit rate, streaming, and HD audio can contribute to your digital audio sample's quality and to its data footprint.

In the next chapter, you learn about **digital audio data footprint optimization** concepts, terms, and principles.

CHAPTER 5

■ ■ ■

The Cleanup of Digital Audio: Noise Removal

Now that you know about some of the different areas of digital audio, including MIDI, synthesis, digital audio recording/sampling, digital audio streaming, captive digital audio, and digital audio data file formats, the next step in the sampling process is to remove those **background noise** "artifacts" from the data sample that you created in Chapter 3. This is especially important when working with voice-overs and similar vocal-oriented samples, because you want it to be relatively quiet—except when the person is speaking, of course.

In this chapter, you learn about the noise removal algorithms in Audacity, which were recoded and taken to a new professional level in version 2.1. Noise reduction is a timely topic for Audacity 2 users.

Noise Removal: Algorithmic Processing

In this chapter, you delve into the process of **background noise removal**, which is the first step you generally take after sampling something. You'll need extra waveform noise as an input to the noise reduction (noise removal) algorithm; this is something that you want to do before you trim the unused portions of your sample. You learn about trimming in the next chapter.

Background noise can come from a significant number of different sources, which is why professional recording studios have rooms with sound-absorbing foam on the walls and that use extremely expensive microphones on stands behind circular pop-screens that prevent vocal pops, like you have at the end of the word "fundamentals" in the current sample. The noise in my sample was recorded on a consumer-quality microphone.

Noise Reduction: Defining the Background Noise

If you play the CH3.aud digital audio sample created in Chapter 3, and you listen carefully, you can hear background noise.

This is especially evident at the beginning and the end of the data sample. If you do not have Audacity open, launch it and open the **CH3.aud** project file now, so that you can learn

---

Electronic supplementary material The online version of this chapter
(doi:10.1007/978-1-4842-1648-4_5) contains supplementary material, which is available to authorized users.

how to fix this problem using the Audacity **noise reduction algorithm**. It's unprofessional to have background noise in the digital audio assets in any of your applications.

Now you begin to get experience in using your Audacity **Effect** menu to apply digital audio sample processing effects; in this case, to remove background noise.

The work process for removing noise in Audacity—perfect for use with voice-over tracks—involves using the vertical bar tool to select a portion of the audio sample that only has noise in it. The easiest way to do this with surgical precision starts with the **Zoom tool**. It is accessed by selecting the **magnifying glass icon**, which is next to the record button. Click the vocal waveform one or two times to zoom into the sample data so that you can see the voice data in the waveform, as shown in Figure 5-1.

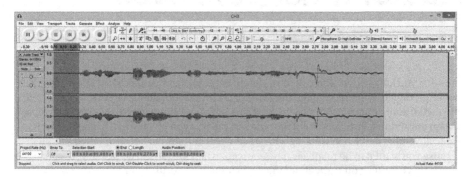

Figure 5-1. *Select an area with noise, using the vertical bar icon*

The noise reduction algorithm uses the noise data that you select; the most logical sample is the data before the first word starts. The noise reduction algorithm can use it to develop algorithmic noise data "profiles" and then remove similar noise across your entire data sample.

After you define noise in the algorithm, the next step processes the entire waveform and removes similar noise data from your audio sample.

As you can see in Figure 5-1, I've zoomed in and selected a section of the sample data that has noise in it, using the vertical bar (waveform selection) tool, which is located right next to the record button.

Be careful not to select any portion of your sound wave that contains vocal content.

Next, in the **Effect** menu, select the **Noise Reduction** algorithm option, as shown in Figure 5-2.

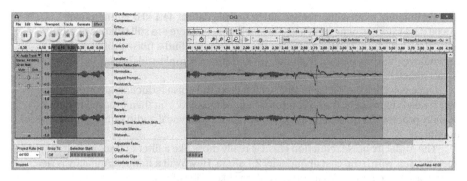

Figure 5-2. *Select the Effect menu and Noise Reduction submenu*

This opens the **Noise Reduction** dialog (see Figure 5-3), where you click the **Get Noise Profile** button. I selected only a quarter of a second of noise data, even though Step 1 of the dialog advises you to select a few seconds of isolated noise data, which may not be possible.

Noise Reduction ✕

Step 1

Select a few seconds of just noise so Audacity knows what to filter out, then click Get Noise Profile:

> Get Noise Profile

Step 2

Select all of the audio you want filtered, choose how much noise you want filtered out, and then click 'OK' to reduce noise.

Noise reduction (dB):	12
Sensitivity:	6.00
Frequency smoothing (bands):	0

Noise: ◉ Reduce ◯ Residue

Preview   OK   Cancel

Figure 5-3. *Click the Get Noise Profile button then click on OK*

Fortunately, even a quarter-second of sample data at 44.1 kHz contains over 11,000 data samples of noise at a 32-bit resolution, so there are still trillions of bits of noise data. This is certainly enough for the algorithm to find a noise profile so that it can remove this data pattern from the rest of the data sample and (hopefully) leave the vocals intact.

Once you click Get Noise Profile, which gives the noise reduction algorithm the data it needs to process, the **OK** button becomes enabled. You then proceed to Step 2 to actually process the noise data and remove it from your vocal audio sample, hopefully in its entirety.

The Audacity noise reduction effect is really more like a filter in the way that it operates; it is worth the cost of Audacity 2.1 alone. Hey! Wait a minute! Audacity is free! Sorry about that, I forgot, as it certainly seems like paid software.

Noise Reduction: Removing the Background Noise

Make sure to deselect any selected portion of your sound wave before applying the noise reduction algorithm, because only the selected section will be processed. This is quite handy to know when selective noise reduction is what you want to achieve. I used the following default settings for my initial noise reduction algorithm "pass": a **Noise Reduction** of 12 decibels, a **Sensitivity** of 6, and the **Frequency smoothing bands** at 0, as shown in Figure 5-3.

As you can see in Figure 5-4, the algorithm did a fairly good job of removing the background noise in my voice-over data sample.

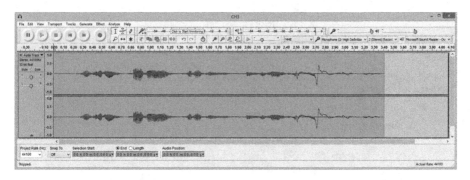

Figure 5-4. *Deselect the waveform and apply the default setting*

Play the audio sample using the green **play** icon in the control transport, seen in the top-left corner of Figure 5-4. Listen carefully for any background hiss. I don't hear too much hissing in the first part of this sample; however, there is hissing in the second part (end) of the data sample.

To improve the noise reduction result, you may need more extreme settings than the defaults suggested by Audacity in this dialog. The process for doing this includes using the **Edit ➤ Undo Noise Reduction** menu sequence, and subsequently trying different decibels, sensitivity, and frequency smoothing settings in Step 2 of the Noise Reduction dialog.

Let's go through the work process that I used to get better noise reduction results. The first thing I tried was a higher decibel setting, so I doubled the 12 decibels to 24.

I saved the different results using the lossless FLAC audio data format so that you can hear the results that I hear as I refine these settings. I named the files **CH5-decibel-sensitivity-smoothing.FLAC** so that the audio file names show the actual dialog settings used.

I used FLAC because it is lossless, so you can reproduce the exact same data bytes that I have in my system by importing these files into Audacity 2.1.1 using the **File ➤ Import ➤ Audio ➤ FLAC** menu (and dialog drop-down setting) command sequence.

Using 24 decibels further reduced the noise level, but also introduced a slight chirping effect near the end of the sample. I decided to double this setting again, to the maximum 48 decibels setting, to see if this exacerbated the chirping and if it would also reduce background noise levels even further.

The 48 decibels setting did indeed remove more background noise, but the chirping effect on the word fundamentals remained the same, so I decided to stay at 48 decibels.

I then started to refine my default Sensitivity setting to see if I could get an even better result. I doubled this setting to 12 to see if it would reduce the chirping effect. The sample didn't sound much different, so I maxed the setting out at 24.

The chirping sounded worse with decibels and sensitivity maxed out, so I tried the other extreme and set the Sensitivity to 0, which entirely turned off the noise reduction algorithm!

This setting tells the noise reduction algorithm the amount of sensitivity to apply to the data sample; that is, how sensitive the effects are to the sound wave. Since it's called "Sensitivity," this is logical, if you think about it. I found that a Sensitivity setting of 4 minimized the chirping effects.

Next, I started applying the **Frequency smoothing bands** settings (0 through 6). The more I increased the frequency smoothing, the more the vocals became "muddied"; thus, I decided to use a setting of 0 or 1. Frequency smoothing affects the **sharpness** (clarity) of a sound wave, just as smoothing (blur) does in a digital image.

You can see the different results by using the FLAC files that I include with this book, or you can simply try it out on your own vocal sample to get a feel for the settings.

Figure 5-5 shows my FLAC files for some of the primary noise reduction settings that I tried, which I exported as FLAC files, along with the original noisy source file as a baseline; you can see the amount of data that the noise reduction took out of the original sample, which came in at 316 kilobytes.

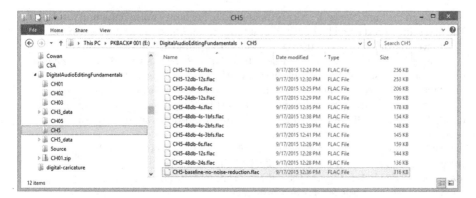

Figure 5-5. *Noise reduction data shown as numbers by using FLAC*

This approach, which is a glimpse of things to come in Chapter 12, allows you to see how the amount of data removed by the noise reduction algorithm relates numerically across all of the settings.

This provides you with an alternate way of analyzing the result of the noise reduction algorithm, instead of looking at your sampled waveform data representation inside of Audacity.

Now that your waveform is cleaned up a bit, in the next chapter, you can learn how to trim away some of the unnecessary parts of the data sample.

Summary

In this chapter, you looked at digital audio sample noise-reduction concepts, principles, and work processes. You learned how to give the Audacity noise reduction algorithm a sample of your noise data and how to work with noise reduction decibel, sensitivity, and frequency smoothing band settings.

In the next chapter, you learn about **digital audio sample editing**, including **scrubbing** and **trimming** operations.

■ ■ ■

CHAPTER 6

The Isolation of Digital Audio: Trimming Tools

Now that you have removed the noise from the background of your voice-over, it is time to look at how to trim it up so that the unneeded audio—such as the intro and exit unused dead space—can be eliminated. Doing this reduces the data footprint and makes the audio trigger with more surgical precision.

You'll also look at how to extract individual words, in case you want to make a game where your character talks using individual words. And you'll learn about "scrubbing" audio and how to play waveforms backward, among other fun endeavors.

Audio Sample Editing: Basic Techniques

In this chapter, I'll show you some of the basic ways to extract the sound waves that you need to isolate and utilize in your multimedia production, whether that be creating podcast content, web sites, audio eBooks, Android applications, iTV shows, digital videos, or similar digital new media that incorporates digital audio in one way or another.

The primary reason to trim away any unused "dead space" in your samples is to increase your "response time" once you load your data samples into a sampler, sample playback software, or your own custom C, Java, JavaScript, or HTML5 code that triggers (play) your samples.

If you kept the dead space in the sample that you cleaned up in Chapter 5 (even though this dead space is now quiet and more professional), it will cause a **delay** if your data sample is triggered by the user interface in your web site, application, iTV program, or sample playback engine. This will seem less than professional to end users. Therefore, you need to isolate the usable parts of a sample and let the application using the sample control the timing (the dead space) among your different audio samples.

Electronic supplementary material The online version of this chapter (doi:10.1007/978-1-4842-1648-4_6) contains supplementary material, which is available to authorized users.

Trimming Digital Audio: Removing Unused Data

There are five digital audio editing icons on the right side of the Audacity window, located underneath the audio playback level meter that controls the **cut**, **copy**, **paste**, **trim**, and **silence** editing functions. Since the first logical step is to remove the dead space before and after your voice-over, let's look at the trim tool first. Select the portion of the data sample that contains vocal data (see Figure 6-1) and click the **Trim Audio** icon (circled in red, with the tool tip pop-up shown on mouse-over).

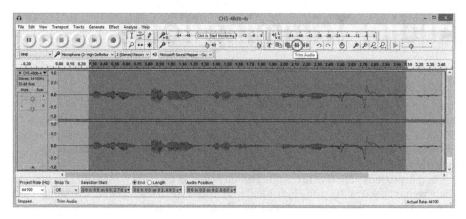

Figure 6-1. *Select the voice-over part of the vocal sample data*

This removes the dead space; however, it still leaves the delay coming into your data sample, as you can see on the left of Figure 6-1 in light gray. To move your samples back to 0, go to **Tracks ➤ Align Tracks ➤ Start to Zero**, as shown in Figure 6-2. This eliminates the dead space coming into the data sample, so that when your application triggers the sample, audio playback response is immediate.

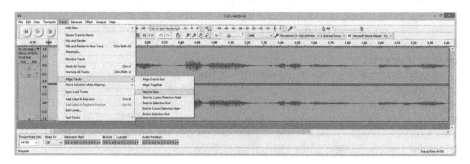

Figure 6-2. *Use Tracks ➤ Align Tracks ➤ Start to Zero function*

Besides Noise Removal, which needs the noise data in the dead space (and why you did that process pre-trim), trimming your data sample is one of those things you do "up front" during your sample recording and editing work process. Now the voice-over of the book title can be triggered in a project and it will immediately say the book title when triggered.

Next, let's drill down a level deeper to see how you can extract the individual words in the voice-over, in case you need finer control over each of the words spoken.

Extracting Audio: Selecting Sample Components

As you can see on the left side of Figure 6-3, you can select a portion of the waveform (in this case, the word **audio**) and click the **play** button in the transport (shown depressed) and play only the selected portion of the sample. You can tell that the data sample portion is playing by looking at the vertical bar (a **playback head**) in the middle of the selected area and the output level meters.

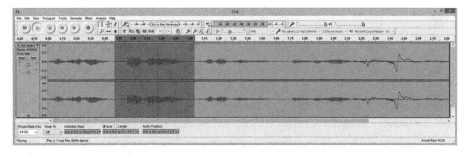

Figure 6-3. *Select the portion of the sample you want to play*

Once you have fine-tuned your selection until it reaches the subsample result that you wanted to achieve, you can use another useful feature with this selection, which allows you to save this subsample as its own separate data sample.

You can record vocabulary for the application and apply noise reduction in one pass, and later simply use this select-and-export work process to create an audio data sample in any of a dozen data formats supported by Audacity 2.1.1 by using the LAME and FFMPEG libraries.

The menu sequence that you will use to achieve this result is the **File ➤ Export Selected Audio** work process, seen on the left side of Figure 6-4 and selected in light blue.

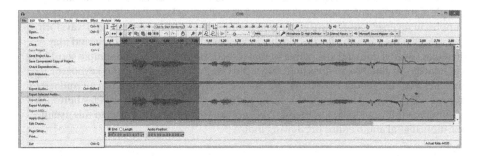

Figure 6-4. *Use File ➤ Save Selected Audio to create sub-sample*

Once you select the menu sequence, you see the **Export Selected Audio** dialog, where you select the digital audio data format. As you can see in Figure 6-5, I'm using the FLAC audio format for the assets for the book, because it gives me 100% perfect reproduction of the waveforms used in this book, along with at least a 50% lower data footprint than what the uncompressed PCM format would give me. More on this later in Chapter 12.

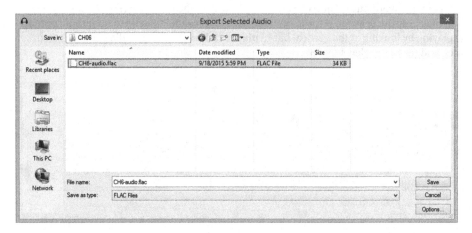

Figure 6-5. *Use Export Selected Audio dialog and name CH6-audio*

Next, let's take a look at another recent feature upgrade for Audacity 2.1—real-time, **bi-directional**, digital audio data sample **scrubbing**!

This is not really scrubbing (cleaning) the audio sample data, else I would have put it in the audio clean-up chapter! I think you will find this particular feature both useful as well as fun to use, as it allows fine-tuned sample playback control.

Scrubbing Digital Audio: Sample Playback Rate

Another feature that Audacity upgraded considerably in version 2.1 is real-time audio sample scrubbing, which now works forward as well as backward, so that you can play samples in reverse! This feature allows you to drag your cursor over the audio waveforms and see what they are, change the playback rate based on how fast you drag, and play them backward if you drag the cursor in that direction. To enable audio sample scrubbing in Audacity, all you have to do is hold down the Control (**Ctrl**) key on your keyboard, and click your left mouse button. As you can see in Figure 6-6, this turns on an Audacity transport Play button; to turn off this feature, simply click the (depressed) Play button. It's as simple as that, and fairly fun to use. Try it now so that you can get used to this useful, real-time digital audio editor previewing tool.

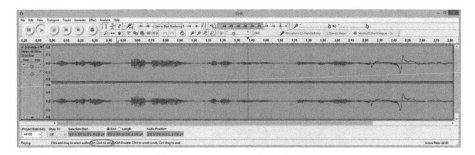

Figure 6-6. *Use Ctrl-Click to enable the data scrubbing function*

Next, let's take a look at how to re-arrange the order of the title of the book inside the voice-over waveform by using the cut, copy, and paste features in Audacity 2.1.1.

Rearranging Digital Audio: Cut, Copy, and Paste

Let's pretend that the title of this book is "Editing Digital Audio: Fundamentals," and that I recorded the vocal sample incorrectly. The work process for correcting this using Audacity editing tools involves selecting the word "Editing" with an even margin of silence around it, removing that section from the audio data sample, moving the cursor to time location 0.00, and pasting the section at the front of the voice-over sample.

Select the vocal portion representing the word "editing" and leave some of the silence margin on the right side (end) of the subsample, as shown selected in blueish-gray in Figure 6-7. Play the selected portion using the **play** button, and then click the **scissor icon** to remove the sample data.

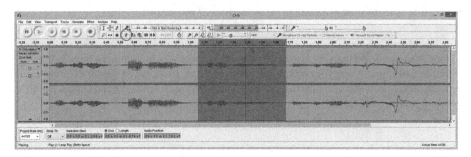

Figure 6-7. *Select a sample for the word "editing," and preview*

I circled the **cut** (scissor) tool in Figure 6-7. Figure 6-8 shows the result, with the insertion (position) bar sitting right where the editing vocal used to be.

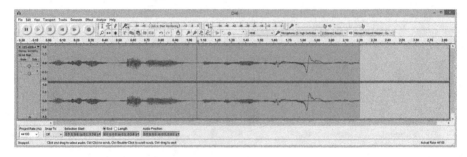

Figure 6-8. *Sample data for "editing" removed from data sample*

The next step in the work process is to position the bar at position **0.00**, which you can do by clicking the vertical bar tool. You can make sure that you're at 0.00 by using the **Edit ➤ Move Cursor ➤ to Track Start** feature, seen in Figure 6-9 on the left-hand side of the screen.

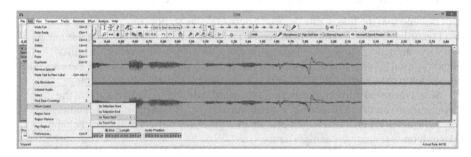

Figure 6-9. *Use the Edit ➤ Move Cursor ➤ to Track Start feature*

The **Move Cursor** submenu options allow you to perform surgically correct edits, so familiarize yourself with them now so that you know where to find these basic but valuable tools for aligning your editing "moves." Figure 6-10 shows the result of the work process. And now when you play the sample, it correctly states the "Editing Digital Audio Fundamentals" book title.

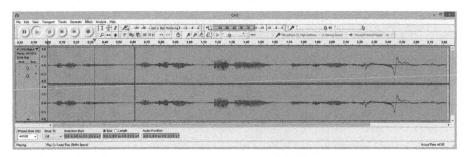

Figure 6-10. *Vocal is now "Editing Digital Audio Fundamentals"*

Practice using these fundamental digital audio editing tools in Audacity, because this forms a foundation for the workflow in your digital audio work process as a multimedia producer or a digital audio engineer.

Summary

In this chapter, you looked at digital audio data-editing–related concepts and principles, such as trimming audio samples, extracting audio subsamples, and rearranging audio subsamples. You also looked at how your resolution, color channels, color depth, and alpha channel can contribute to data footprint reduction.

In the next chapter, you learn about **manual digital audio sample editing** concepts, techniques, and work processes.

CHAPTER 7

■ ■ ■

The Manual Labor of Digital Audio: Sample Editing

You now know how to trim unused space around your sample so that it triggers more surgically. You also know how to have Audacity position the digital audio editing insertion point for you and how you can move portions of your sample around with the cut, copy, and paste functions. Now let's look at how to edit and affect the sample data itself by removing those high-pitched "chirping" artifacts that were introduced from using the noise reduction algorithm in Chapter 5.

This chapter explores how to find isolated chirps using tools such as **zoom**, **select**, and **preview**, and how to replace these chirps using the **silence audio** function. You will see how to **algorithmically remove** several chirps (artifacts) that exist in the second half of the sample. These sample artifacts are fused together with, or are a part of, the vocal sound wave itself.

Audio Data Editing: Changing the Sample

In this chapter, you are going to change the digital audio sample data so that it actually sounds different. Don't worry, you are going to make it sound better by removing the chirps caused by applying the noise reduction algorithm. I call these **artifacts**, as they are a side effect of algorithmic processing.

One example of a visual artifact is image data degradation, initiated by JPEG (image) or MPEG (video) compression algorithms and causing a discolored area (usually green, purple, or yellow) of pixels to appear in parts of the image or video. Chirps are the aural equivalent of this, and they are especially noticeable, so I am going to tell you how to remove these. Doing this also gives you more practice with the fundamental editing tools in Audacity, and introduces you to another Effect menu tool because some of these artifacts (chirps) are isolated and some are integrated within the audio sample waveforms.

Electronic supplementary material The online version of this chapter (doi:10.1007/978-1-4842-1648-4_7) contains supplementary material, which is available to authorized users.

Cleaning the Sample: Removing Isolated Artifacts

You can find isolated chirp artifacts either by **scrubbing** (a feature you learned about in Chapter 6) or by playing the entire sample by clicking the **play** button and watching the position of the **vertical line** that shows where in the sample Audacity is playing that audio from, which is how I did it. Once you think you see the artifact, select the area of the sample containing the artifact, and again use the play button to preview just the selected area to see if this in indeed the artifact that you've selected. Figure 7-1 shows this along with the **silence audio icon**, which I circled in red. Clicking the silence audio icon removes the first of the chirping artifacts.

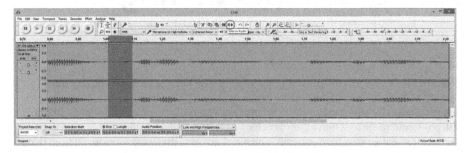

Figure 7-1. *Select the first artifact and preview it*

Find the next isolated chirp artifact, and again, select it and click the **play** button to preview only the artifact, as shown in Figure 7-2. You can tell I am previewing sample audio by the **level meters** on the right side of the screenshot. Notice in Figures 7-1 and 7-2 that this artifact looks more like a rectangle than a sound waveform, which is a clue that it is a tone, chirp, or pulse of some sort.

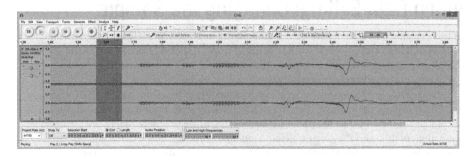

Figure 7-2. *Select a second artifact, and preview it*

If you also want to see the artifact visually, there's a **View ➤ Fit in Window** menu sequence as well as the **Fit Selection** icon, shown circled in red at the top of Figure 7-3. Notice that I removed the artifact in the selected area shown in Figure 7-2 (when the chirp artifact was still intact).

48

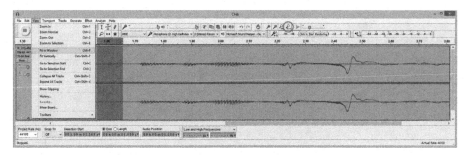

Figure 7-3. *You can zoom into a selection, using Fit in Window*

Now that you have removed your isolated chirp artifacts, which are the easiest to locate, the next level of complexity is to remove the chirps that are actually **attached to** these sample waveforms. Let's take a look at how this is done.

Sample Data Surgery: Removing Attached Artifacts

As you were previewing the entire data sample, you probably noticed that there was a chirp artifact on the front part of the word "audio." This subsample is shown selected in Figure 7-4, along with the **Fit Selection** icon, shown circled in red. I clicked the icon to fit the selection into the Audacity editor area so that I could see what I was doing while I extracted the artifact, which again has **no waveform variation** and seems to have the same rectangular shape as the other artifacts. I did this using 100% zooming of the data sample.

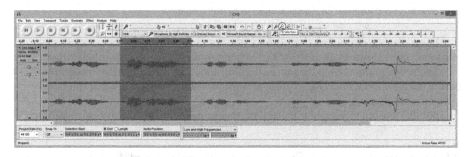

Figure 7-4. *Select only your vocal sample for the word "audio"*

Select the data that represents the chirp artifact. This is the first part of the waveform, shown zoomed in on the left side of Figure 7-5. Use the **play** button to preview it, make sure that this is the chirp, and then use the **Silence Audio** icon to remove it. You can see by the selection area that I ascertained where the vocal waveform should start by looking at the **pattern** of the wave (seen to the right of the selection area). I made the end point of the selection area match up with this waveform so that the pattern was consistent through the subsample.

49

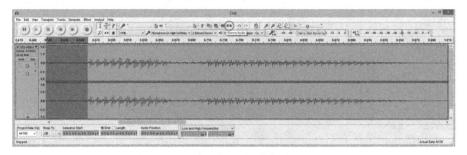

Figure 7-5. *Zoom into subsample and select the chirp artifact*

As you can see in Figure 7-6, the Silence Audio function removed the chirp artifact and the "audio" subsample looks much cleaner. It now sounds absolutely clear. It is perfect.

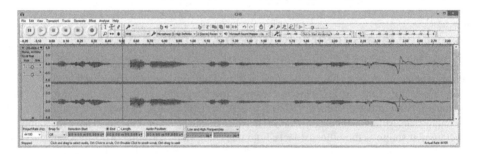

Figure 7-6. *A rectangular chirp artifact is surgically removed*

If you play the entire data sample back, the first half of this voice-over sounds clean and intelligible. However, the second half of the sample still has that chirping artifact.

The problem now is that the remaining chirping tones are actually an **integrated part** of the waveform, not isolated areas or segments of the sound wave that can be selected and removed.

For this reason, to finish the artifact removal process, you need to use an algorithm.

Algorithmic Sample Surgery: Integrated Artifacts

To remove the rest of the chirp artifacts, you need something that can analyze the components of your sample waveform and that can extract these higher frequency chirps algorithmically. Fortunately, Audacity has something called **Vocal Reduction and Isolation** in the Effect menu. Sometimes the best approach is to do the opposite of what you want to achieve in an editing move; instead of trying to isolate the chirp, let's isolate the voice!

Figure 7-7 shows the **Effect** menu and the Vocal Reduction and Isolation option and dialog. I cut the menu in half to fit it into one screenshot because Audacity currently has a problem (they are working on it) with the Effect menu being too long due to so many cool Audacity effects. It's a great problem to have, if you ask me!

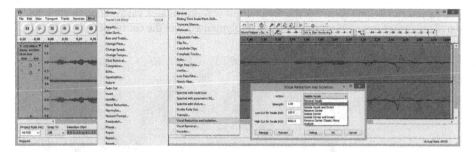

Figure 7-7. *Use the Effect ➤ Vocal Reduction and Isolation menu*

I tried the default settings in the **Vocal Reduction and Isolation** dialog, as I always do, but the **High Cut** (which controls the high pitch you are trying to eliminate) setting of 9000 Hz (9 kHz) is too high to eliminate this chirping artifact.

My process was to reduce this number by 1000, and I therefore tried 8000, and then 7000, and then 6000, and finally 5000, but I still heard evidence of the chirping artifact.

Next, I tried 4000. This eliminated the chirp artifact but also affected (muddied) the vocal tones, so I added 100 back on the 4000 value at that point; ultimately, 4500 (half the suggested value) was the value that eliminated the chirping artifact and it didn't affect the vocals too perceptibly.

I did try 4600 just to make sure, but heard the chirping artifact at that setting, so I decided to stay with a High Cut setting of 4500 Hz (4.5 kHz) as my final setting. I left a full-strength algorithm application (default) setting of 100% and a **Low Cut** setting of 120 Hz, as I was not trying to remove a lower pitch artifact. You could also set the Low Cut setting to 0.

Figure 7-8 shows the selected portion of this waveform, as well as the Vocal Reduction and Isolation dialog and final settings.

Figure 7-8. *Set the High Cut data field to 4500 Hz and click OK*

Also notice that the Vocal Reduction and Isolation dialog has a **Preview** button so that you can preview your settings in real time. If you enter a number into one of the three data fields, and then click **Preview**, this has the same effect as hitting your Enter key, which "enters" the data value in the data field.

As you can see in Figure 7-9, the data sample waveforms look vastly different after the significant waveform editing "moves" were implemented over the course of the chapter.

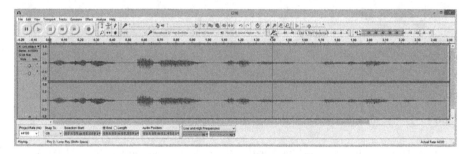

Figure 7-9. *The algorithm processed sub-sample looks far better*

Clearly, those sci-fi-sounding, high-pitch chirp artifacts were contained in that wild-looking tail at the end of the data sample (see Figure 7-8) and that have now been eliminated by using the Audacity Vocal Reduction and Isolation filter (effect) algorithmic processor (see Figure 7-9). As you might suspect, this data sample probably is a lot less to compress.

Let's take a look at just how much less data the cleaned-up sample takes than the original 316 KB data sample. This will be the primary focus of the data footprint optimization chapter, as you may have guessed. This is because noise and artifacts are difficult to compress.

Removing noise and artifacts may significantly reduce the data footprint a; in this case, it was approximately 300%, which is amazing if you ask me.

If something is accomplished in this book that has a significant effect on the data footprint, I would be remiss not to point it out or to explain the reasons why it happened.

As you can see in Figure 7-10, when I utilized the **File ➤ Export Audio** menu sequence and dialog, I got a 112 KB FLAC file, which is about three times, or 300% smaller than the 316 KB baseline file that I saved after I recorded the original data sample back in Chapter 5. You can refer to Figure 5-5 if you need to.

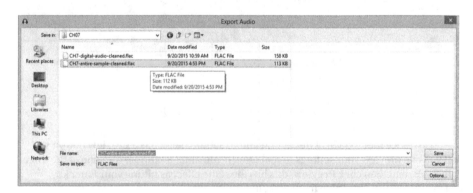

Figure 7-10. *Exporting the cleaned sample using the FLAC format*

You've now cleaned up and greatly reduced the data for this vocal sample, using manual editing tools and the noise reduction and the vocal reduction and isolation algorithms.

Summary

In this chapter, you explored the process of editing the data sample to change how it sounds. In this case, the objective was to remove the chirping artifacts from Chapter 5, where you learned how to remove background noise. Since then you have learned how to use the silence audio tool, which is an alternate work process to using the noise reduction algorithm. You looked at how to select and preview audio to find artifacts, how to have Audacity align the insertion (position) indicator using the **silence audio** tool, and how to remove artifacts algorithmically using the **Vocal Reduction and Isolation** tool.

In the next chapter, you learn about **algorithmic digital audio data processing** concepts, tools, and techniques.

CHAPTER 8

■ ■ ■

The Algorithms of Digital Audio: Audio Processing

Now that you have an understanding of the hands-on digital audio editing tools in Audacity, it's time to look at how you can use **algorithms**, which take the form of **plug-in filters** and **effects**, to apply waveform editing operations and special effects with math and code routines.

You'll look at a number of the primary audio editing and "sweetening" effects in the Audacity 2.1 Effect menu. Some of them visualize the concepts that you learned about in the first few chapters of the book. This offers reinforcement of the principles. You will learn how to utilize algorithms that allow you to amplify waveforms, shift the pitch, change the playback speed, equalize the frequency response, and apply audio effects such as reverb and echo (delay). You also learn how to selectively filter frequencies out of your sample waveform by using audio filters such as High Pass, Low Pass, and Notch Filters.

Audacity 2.1 has 44 default Effect menu entries, so I can't cover them all in this chapter. I'll cover the ones that demonstrate the concepts you have already learned, and some of the others that are editing mainstays; so you'll learn all the basic processing.

It's important to note that there are another 80 plug-in filters that you can add to the Effect menu by using **Effect ➤ Manage**, shown at the top of the Effect menu in Figure 8-1.

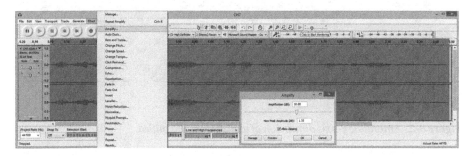

Figure 8-1. *Select sample and use an Effect ➤ Amplify algorithm*

Electronic supplementary material The online version of this chapter (doi:10.1007/978-1-4842-1648-4_8) contains supplementary material, which is available to authorized users.

Algorithmic Audio Effects Processing

Algorithms are code (usually C++ in digital audio editing) that process your sample waveform. This is why it is important that you use a high-quality sampling frequency—at least CD quality (44.1 kHz) or THX quality (48 kHz)—and leave the sample resolution at 32 bits until the editing and processing is done and you are ready to perform data footprint optimization.

The reason for using the highest possible sampling frequency and sample resolution is that you want to give as much data to the algorithm as you possibly can. The more data the algorithm has, the better results it can provide. Later, after all the processing is complete, you can reduce your sample resolution to 24-bit (HD), or more likely to 16-bit, which is CD quality. You can preview using your ears, your eyes (waveform), and even a data result (export audio as PCM or FLAC), as you've seen in previous chapters and will see in this chapter.

Waveform Amplitude: The Amplify Effect

The first effect that you apply increases the y-axis dimension in the amplitude of the waveform. The result of this is amplification, more commonly referred to as "turning up the volume." Open your **CH7.aud** Audacity project and select the entire waveform, as is shown in Figure 8-1. Select **Effect ➤ Amplify** and enter an amplification factor in decibels; I used 10.6, which is a 133% peak amplitude (a 1.33 factor). Next, select the **Allow clipping** option. You can also use the Preview button to preview different settings until you find one that sounds good to you.

Once you click the **OK** button to apply an Amplify effect, you are able to see this effect algorithmically applied to your waveform. This is shown in Figure 8-2, and as you can see, the waveform looks (and sounds) drastically different.

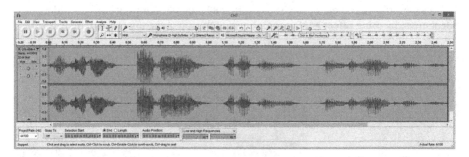

Figure 8-2. *Amplitude y-axis dimension of waveform is magnified*

The sample is indeed louder on playback; however, as you can hear, the quality is lower. I don't hear any artifact introduction, but the clarity of the vocals has suffered, so I used the **Edit ➤ Undo Amplify** menu sequence to undo the algorithm processing. I will tell my app users to turn up their volume.

If you look at the amplified data sample waveform shown in Figure 8-2, it is obvious that this sample waveform has been stretched (only) along the y axis, which is the **amplitude** (volume) of your sample. This effect reinforces what you learned about audio sample characteristics in Chapter 3.

Next, let's take a look at the x axis, or frequency, of the waveform. Changing the frequency of your waveform is called **pitch shifting**.

Waveform Frequency: The Pitch Shifting Effect

Next, let's take a look at the other sample characteristic that you learned about in Chapter 3, sample frequency. To change your data sample frequency, you use the **Effect ➤ Change Pitch** menu sequence, which is shown on the left side of Figure 8-3. I shifted the pitch up one octave, or 100%, so that my vocal sounds like a member of the popular chipmunk trio.

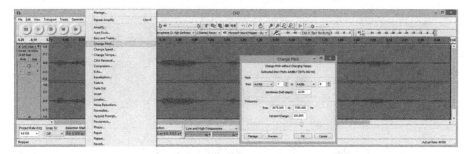

Figure 8-3. *Select sample, then Effect ➤ Change Pitch algorithm*

As you can see in the **Change Pitch** dialog, there are 12 semitones to an octave, and the **Percent Change** data field shows that there is a 100% full octave pitch increase indicated.

If you are sampling notes using an instrument that is in tune, you can also select pitch changes by notes. I clicked the **OK** button to apply the algorithm. This time, the x axis of the sampled waveform was affected and the amount of data was doubled in this dimension, creating a waveform twice as dense, as you can see in Figure 8-4.

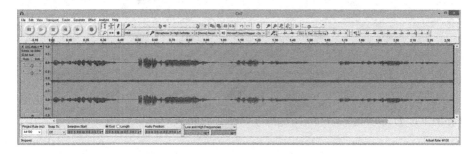

Figure 8-4. *Frequency x-axis dimension of sample is compressed*

Since I'm not currently working on a chipmunks movie or games, I used the **Edit ➤ Undo Change Pitch** menu sequence to return to the original data sample waveform.

Waveform Speed: Vinyl Record Playback Speeds

An algorithm similar to the Change Pitch effect is the **Change Speed** effect (see Figure 8-5). It does much the same thing to your frequency (the x axis) without keeping the sample length (time) the same. What this does is shorten the (time) length for your sample. Interestingly, the paradigm that the Change Speed dialog uses is old-fashioned vinyl record RPMs! The baseline is large 33.3 RPM records with options to change the playback speed to match a 45 RMP record, or even an ancient 78 RPM record. As you can see, the dialog also allows you to specify speed adjustment using a multiplier, percentage, or actual time value, all of which are calculated in real time.

Figure 8-5. *Select sample, then Effect ➤ Change Speed algorithm*

As you can see in Figure 8-6, your data sample waveforms are compressed along the x axis like they were in Change Pitch, but the sample is shorter (rather than length being maintained), as you can see on the right. This 35% change is the amount of gray shown on the right in Figure 8-6; you can see the multiplier and percent change numbers that you specified in the dialog visually inside the Audacity 2.1.1 application.

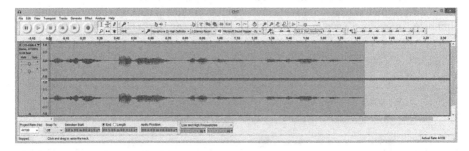

Figure 8-6. *Frequency x axis and length of sample is compressed*

Next, let's look at one of the more complex algorithms, **Equalization**; it has a more detailed user interface. This effect is a lot of fun to tweak, and with a visual UI, it is fairly easy to use. Equalization is one of the more popular audio effects among consumers, as is evidenced by the large numbers of stereos that come equipped with equalization sliders.

Waveform Equalization: The Equalization Algorithm

If you want to equalize your digital audio sample, you can use the Audacity Equalization (EQ) effect. It permanently applies an EQ setting to your audio data, so make sure that no one else plans to put their EQ settings on top of yours! As you can see in Figure 8-7, the dialog for this effect can be very involved.

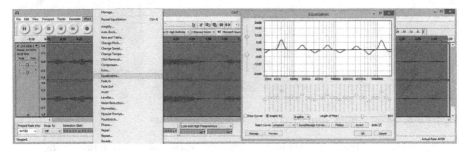

Figure 8-7. *Select sample, then Effect ➤ Equalization algorithm*

The easiest (and most familiar) mode in the user interface is the Graphic EQ mode. Select the **Graphic EQ** radio button and let the Equalization dialog draw the curves for you, as shown in Figure 8-7.

As you can see, the Equalization dialog is very powerful. It offers fine-tuned adjustment of any frequency. You can add to or subtract from any of 32 different frequencies.

The best way to work with this effect is to use your ears to preview your slider settings as frequently as you can. This is made easy with the Preview button, shown highlighted in blue in the lower left of the dialog shown in Figure 8-7.

The two sliders on the left, as well as the **Length of Filter** slider on the bottom of the dialog, allow you to fine-tune the frequency grid display that the spline curves will be drawn on top of. If you want to learn more about spline curves, check out my *Android Studio New Media Fundamentals* (Apress, 2015) book; it covers the fundamentals of all five of the new media genres.

You can save equalization curve collections with presets by using the **Save/Manage Curves** feature. You can invert or flatten your curves by using the **Flatten** and **Invert** buttons. You'll find you can also turn off the grid guidelines by deselecting the **Grids** check box, although I recommend that you keep them visible.

Waveform Reverberation: The Reverb Effect

Another popular digital audio effect that is often applied with algorithmic processing is **reverb**. Reverb simulates being inside an enclosure, whether a small room or a large amphitheater. For this reason, a primary setting in the Reverb dialog (see Figure 8-8) is the **Room Size**, which defaults to 75%. There's also a millisecond pre-delay data value that you can provide, as well as **Reverberance**, **Damping**, and **Stereo Width** percentage values. To fine-tune the effect, you can reduce the percentage of low tone and high tone frequencies that get through the filter, and set custom **Wet Gain** or **Dry Gain** values in decibels.

Figure 8-8. *Select sample, and select Effect ➤ Reverb algorithm*

I decided to try the default settings, which provide a standard reverb processing result, to see what the algorithmic processing is going to do to a sample waveform.

As you can see in Figure 8-9, the sample waveform is far more complex than it was before. This means that an effect like reverb is going to influence your data footprint, because there is more data to compress. The areas that were silent (thin lines) have room echo data in them, as you can see over the duration of the entire data sample.

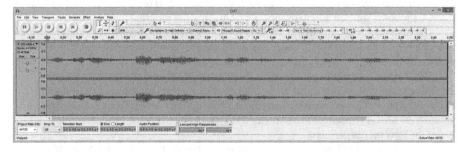

Figure 8-9. *Frequency x axis and length of sample is compressed*

Therefore, if your application doesn't require reverb as a special effect, or more importantly, if the platform that you will deliver on can add that effect to the waveform (like Java and Android), then you do not want to "hard-code" the data inside of your basic sample waveform. This approach allows you to have more flexibility in manipulating audio inside of an application. The core effects that you're looking at in this chapter are available in many open source new-media platform API packages, such as those in Java, JavaFX, and Android Studio.

Next, let's look at another effect that provides the echo processing framework to audio waveforms, the **Delay** effect.

Waveform Echo Chamber: The Delay Effect

Whereas the Reverb effect is a subtle type of echo effect, you can create more pronounced echo effects that are more like the long distance echo effects you get in canyons, for instance, by using the Delay effect. There are several types of delay, such as a regular bouncing ball or a reverse bouncing ball, in the Delay drop-down menu (see Figure 8-10). You can set the delay level and the delay time, and even set a pitch change effect from Pitch/Tempo to Pitch Shift. You can fine-tune this effect by specifying the pitch change for each echo using semitones (as you did in the Change Pitch effect) and the number of echoes to produce.

Figure 8-10. *Select sample, and select Effect ➤ Delay algorithm*

As you can see, I selected the bouncing ball delay type, because I like the delay signature that I hear when I bounce a ball. As you might imagine, this delay effect extends your sample duration because it is adding significant echo data (see Figure 8-11). The black vertical line on the right is the end of what was the original sample length. The more delay time and the higher the number of echoes that you specify, the longer the new data sample (time) length becomes.

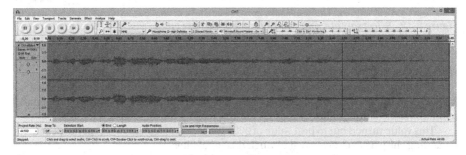

Figure 8-11. *The Delay effect may extend the data sample length*

The Delay effect can add more to the data footprint of a sample than the Reverb effect, so make sure that you need to add echo into your sample; otherwise, find a way to process it "externally" by using Java code, or even OS or hardware capabilities that may provide EQ, reverb, and echo.

Next, let's take a look at how to "shave" frequencies off of your data sample. This is usually done with the Low Pass and the High Pass Filters. You'll use the Low Pass Filter to remove the last remnants of those chirping artifacts you've worked with in the past few chapters. If that doesn't work, there's also a Notch Filter that allows you to target (notch) individual frequencies that you want to filter out or remove from the sample frequency spectrum.

Waveform Shaving: The Low Pass Filter Effect

The High Pass Filter and the Low Pass Filter remove unnecessary frequency data, or frequency data that's undesirable or causing problems with your intended aural result. It can be a good data footprint optimization tool, because even a frequency that cannot be heard needs to be encoded as data, which means that these filters can be used to remove sample data that is not needed (or heard), and thus reduce the data footprint.

As you can see in Figure 8-12, this dialog allows you to specify the **Cutoff frequency**, where everything lower (Low Pass) or higher (High Pass) is "shaved" or removed from the frequency spectrum by the filter's algorithm. There's also the **Rolloff** setting, which specifies the number of decibels per octave that the filter is going to affect. This specifies a magnitude for the application of your cut-off frequency value.

Figure 8-12. *Select sample, and select Effect ➤ Low Pass Filter*

My process for trying to use the Low Pass Filter to remove the last remnants of the chirp artifact was to first use Audacity's default Low Pass Filter settings of 6 dB and 1000 Hz.

This affected the vocal sample and made it duller, so I increased the default cut-off frequency to brighten the vocal sample back up to where it was, while lessening the final remnants of the chirp artifact.

This value turned out to be a value of 2000 Hz, because higher values permitted the remaining chirp artifact to make it through this tonal filter.

After I ascertained the optimal cut-off frequency setting to use, I selected a 12 dB Rolloff option. This provided chirp removal, but it did not affect the vocal data sample quality much.

Finally, I tried a setting of 24 dB, which affected the quality of the vocal part of my data sample too much; so, the final settings for the Low Pass Filter effect were 12 dB and 2000 Hz.

Next, let's take a look at the more surgical Notch Filter, which allows you to specifically target any frequency.

Tunneling Into Your Waveform: The Notch Filter

Instead of cutting off the top or bottom sample waveform frequencies, the Notch Filter effect allows you to surgically "tunnel" into any section of your sample to remove a specific frequency or a range surrounding that frequency. As you can see in Figure 8-13, the **Notch Filter** dialog allows you to specify your target **Frequency** and **Q value**, which is the tunnel width around that frequency. Lower Q values make this tunnel smaller, and so a very small Q value essentially targets the frequency with more surgical precision. The default settings are 60 Hz and a 1.0 Q factor, which I need to change to find the frequencies of the remaining chirp artifacts.

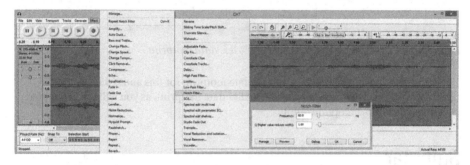

Figure 8-13. *Select sample, and select Effect ➤ Notch Filter*

My process for finding the frequency was to use the Preview button, first at 60 Hz and then at the maximum of 10000 Hz, where the artifact was still audible. Then I used a halfway mark of 5000 Hz, and then backed off that in increments of 1000 until I hit two frequencies that the artifacts were not audible at. These were 3000 Hz and 4000 Hz. I decided to use 4000 Hz because the result sounded better. I left the 100% tunnel size, as you can see in Figure 8-14, and clicked the **OK** button to apply.

Notch Filter	— ▢ ✕
Frequency:	4000.0 ──────⬇────── Hz
Q (higher value reduces width):	1.00 ─⬇────────────────
Manage Preview	Debug OK Cancel

Figure 8-14. *Setting the Notch Filter to a Frequency of 4000 Hz*

63

To see the amount of data that the Notch Filter removed, I targeted the chirp artifact. Then I saved the data sample using the FLAC file format. As you can see in Figure 8-15, the file size is now 104 KB, whereas before it was 112 KB. So, the Notch Filter removed 8 KB worth of artifact data from the sample. The file size is now more than 300% less (104 KB × 3 = 312 KB). The original unedited baseline FLAC file was 316 KB.

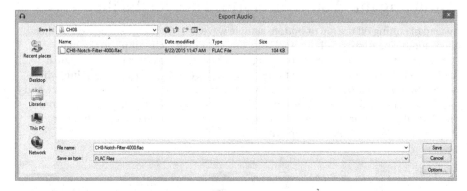

Figure 8-15. *This sample now has over 300% less data footprint*

If the FLAC format is getting a 104 KB data footprint for this audio data sample, other data formats will provide an even smaller data footprint, as you will see in chapter covering data footprint optimization.

Summary

In this chapter, you looked at digital audio processing using algorithms found in the Audacity Effect menu, where internal effects and plug-in filters can be accessed. You looked at many of the mainstream digital audio editing effects that are applied when editing and sweetening digital audio samples. These effects include Amplify, Pitch Shifting, Sample Speed, Equalization, Reverb, Delay, Low Pass Filter, and Notch Filter. You also looked at the **Effect ➤ Manage** menu sequence, which accesses a dialog that allows you to see the other 80 plug-in filters that are not on the Effect menu. Be sure to familiarize yourself with all 128 plug-in filters on the Audacity Effect menu if you want to become a digital audio editing professional.

In the next chapter, you learn about **digital audio data visualization**, by using **spectral analysis** concepts, terms, and principles, along with the Audacity 2.1.1 Analyze menu.

CHAPTER 9

■ ■ ■

A Visualization of Digital Audio: Spectral Analysis

Now that you have an understanding of how to use the Audacity 2 Effect menu to implement algorithmic effects and plug-in filter processing in your digital audio editing, it is time to look at how you should **visualize** the digital audio frequencies that comprise your data sample waveforms.

In this chapter, you'll look at how to visualize waveform frequency distribution using Audacity's **Analyze** menu, along with the **Plot Spectrum** feature, so that you can see exactly what you are doing before and after your digital audio editing "moves," such as the algorithmic processing that you've done in the past several chapters.

You'll look at all the different types of analysis that Audacity can do, including its spectrum analysis features.

Audacity Analyze Menu: Sample Analysis

Audacity's effects and filters aren't the only tools that utilize algorithms; there are also a number of useful audio data analysis tools that use algorithms, which are configured using front-end dialogs, just like the effects and filters featured in Chapters 5–8. There are tools in Audacity's Analyze menu (yes, analysis has its own menu) for contrast (volume) analysis between audio selections, clipping analysis, finding beats, creating label track labels, exporting sample data analysis, and locating silence and the opposite of silence, which are sound samples.

You'll explore several of the most useful tools in the Analyze menu and build on this knowledge in the next few chapters. You'll learn how to generate a **label track** and conform it to vocal samples, how to **export sample analysis**, and how to do **spectral analysis**.

Regular Interval Labels: Automatic Sample Labels

Click the **Analyze** menu at the top right of the Audacity menuing system and look at the eight analysis tools available to do tedious digital audio analysis chores. Select the **Regular Interval Labels** and let Audacity create a label track and insert labels for your vocal subsamples.

Electronic supplementary material The online version of this chapter (doi:10.1007/978-1-4842-1648-4_9) contains supplementary material, which is available to authorized users.

© Wallace Jackson 2015

W. Jackson, *Digital Audio Editing Fundamentals*, DOI 10.1007/978-1-4842-1648-4_9

The Regular Interval Labels dialog is shown in Figure 9-1; it allows you to automate a subsample labeling process. Place your first label at 0.0 [seconds]. In the **Label placement method** drop-down menu, use the **Number of labels** option (set it at 4). Set the **Label text** to vocal. Set the **Minimum number of digits** to None. Set a Yes value for both **Add final label** and **Adjust label interval to fit length**, and then click on **OK**.

Figure 9-1. *Audacity Analyze menu and Regular Interval Labels*

As you can see in Figure 9-2, Audacity created label data in a **Label Track** underneath the Stereo Track, and labeled each vocal using a generic name, *vocal*, and left a data field ready to edit in the first (leftmost) data field, as shown in white at the bottom left of the screenshot. Backspace over the word *vocal* and type **Digital** to rename this first label.

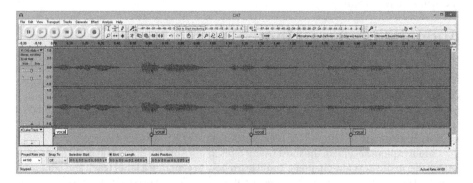

Figure 9-2. *Regular Interval Labels in their own Audacity track*

You can also place your mouse cursor over the dots on the lines that separate these labels, and when they turn white, as shown in the Fundamentals label, click and drag to position the lines where the audio subsamples begin and end, as I have done.

As you can see in Figure 9-3, once you name and position all of the label indicators, you have a great guide for your project, so that others can see what the sample data relates to.

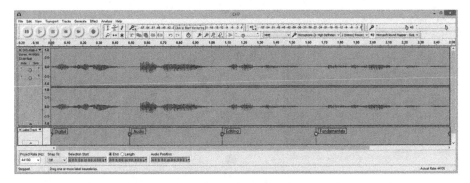

Figure 9-3. *Name and Position label indicators for each sample*

Not only can you drag the dots, which position the lines and arrowheads, but you can also drag each directional arrowhead to define the exact range of the subsample area. I have done this in Figure 9-4 so that you can see how these labels center their text label portions (or try, at least) once you fine-tune their range using the < and > arrowhead icons at the end of each label range in the Label Track.

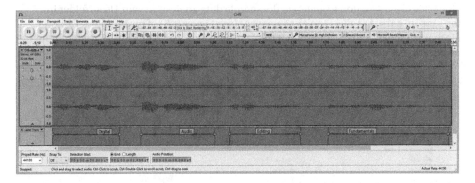

Figure 9-4. *Use label arrowheads, to show sample waveform spans*

Next, let's look at **Sample Data Export**, an Analysis menu function that exports sample data analysis based on the parameters that you give the algorithm.

Sample Data Export: Export Sample Data Analysis

Select the **Analyze** drop-down menu and then select the **Sample Data Export** option (see Figure 9-5). This opens the Sample Data Export dialog, where you can specify the number of samples, the measurement scale, the file data format, the header information to include in the file, the header text, the stereo channel data layout, the file name, the output folder, and the options to show messages and overwrite the data analysis files.

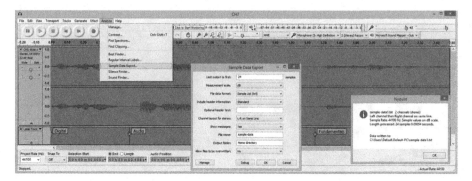

Figure 9-5. *Audacity Analyze menu and Sample Data Export dialog*

I decided to generate 24 data samples using decibels in a Sample List text data format that could be parsed (processed) with code (Java, JavaScript, etc.). I used Standard header information and displayed stereo sample analysis data on the same line. I set **Show messages** to Yes and **Allow files to be overwritten** to No. I named the file **sample-data** and used the default Home directory output folder, which for Windows is the Users folder.

Click the **OK** button to generate the sample data analysis in your Users folder in the sample-data.txt file. I took a screenshot (see Figure 9-6) of my Windows Explorer file management utility, which shows the C:\Users\Default.Default.PC folder for my workstation and a sample-data.txt analysis file.

Figure 9-6. *Find your sample-data.txt file in your Users folder*

I right-clicked the **sample-data.txt** file and selected the **Open with Notepad** (the Windows text editor) option to review the sample analysis data (see Figure 9-7). As you can see in line 18 of the file, there is a decibel spike of 90 for the right channel, where your decibel level is almost twice the normal 45. This is the type of data visualization that the tool provides, along with sample analysis data that can be used in advanced ways in your programming applications.

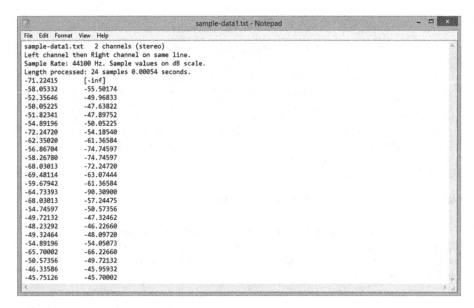

Figure 9-7. View your sample-data.txt file in your text editor

Next, let's look at how you can visualize an audio frequency spectrum that exists inside the audio data sample.

Frequency Spectrum Data Analysis Tools

As you have seen in this book thus far, it can be very difficult to do digital audio editing techniques using only your ears, unless you're one of those few people who have exceptional hearing abilities. For this reason, I have showed you tools or work processes that allow you to visualize sample editing data using file size data, waveforms, and sample data analysis tools. The next Audacity data visualization tool that you are going to learn about is exceptionally powerful, as it allows you to create and view a graph representation of a sample frequency spectrum.

Spectral Analysis: Audacity's Plot Spectrum Dialog

There is a **Plot Spectrum** tool in the Analyze menu that allows you to see the frequency spectrum using algorithm and frequency sampling resolution options. I recommend that you spend some time playing with the **Analyze ➤ Plot Spectrum** function (shown in Figure 9-8) on your own as well, after going through some of the options presented in this chapter.

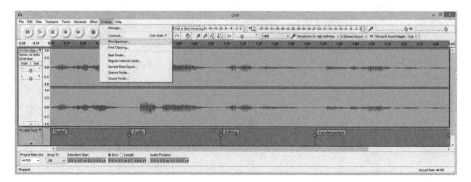

Figure 9-8. *Select the Analyze ➤ Plot Spectrum menu sequence*

As you can see in Figure 9-9, the first thing that I did was visualize the Notch Filter (that you used in Chapter 8) to see if it looks as if I took a notch out of the data sample. As you can clearly see in the right-hand screenshot, there is indeed a clear notch at 4500 Hz. You'll take a look at some of these other settings as well.

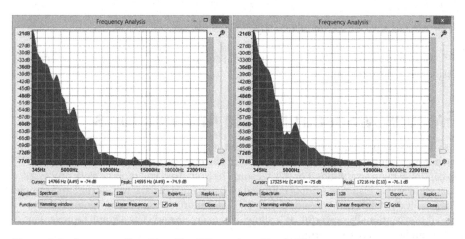

Figure 9-9. *Spectrum Algorithm Size 128, pre/post Notch Filter*

The first thing that you'll look at is how to set the frequency display resolution by using the Frequency Analysis's **Size** drop-down menu. I set it to 256 in the "before" and "after" data samples, so that you can see how it adds more peak data, as the two dialogs show you in Figure 9-10. I'll also show you 512 and 1024 settings later on, so that you can see how these settings visualize your spectrum data.

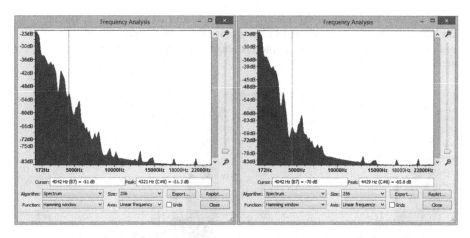

Figure 9-10. *Spectrum Algorithm Size 256, pre/post Notch Filter*

What you have looked at so far is a spectral analysis for your entire data sample; but as you may have surmised, you can also use this tool to analyze subsamples. Let's take a look at that next, as this is an even more useful analysis approach.

Subsample Analysis: Using the Select Tool

Let's select the vocal for Audio, as shown in Figure 9-11. This is made clearer since adding your handy Label Track and the custom label markers that you installed earlier in the chapter. Again, select **Analyze ➤ Plot Spectrum** (see Figure 9-8), which now displays sample data using its algorithms only for the selected data subsample and not for the entire sample. This allows you to only view a subset of the digital audio data that you want to analyze, which also means that there is less data to analyze in the visual graphing function. And, this makes it easier for you to find the audio data that you want to visualize and eventually process. It is analogous to zooming in on an area of a digital image so that you can work only on particular pixels in your digital image. The ability to work with this tool makes it far more powerful.

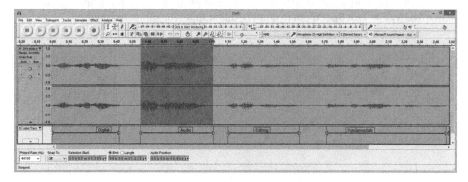

Figure 9-11. *Select vocal for the word audio, above Label Track*

71

In Figure 9-12, you see that I selected a **Size** of 256 and 512 for the notch filtered (the latest version of the voice-over) data sample to show the frequency sampling resolution difference. The higher sample size shows the notch that you carved with increasing precision.

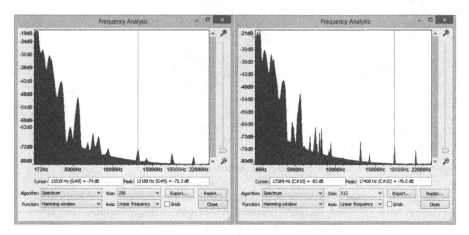

Figure 9-12. *Notch Filter spectral analysis at Size 256 and 512*

It is important to note that the vertical line in your graph should "snap" to the nearest peak as you move your mouse over the data. The **Cursor** and **Peak** readouts provide precise numerical information to use with the Effect menu filters and in their audio effect dialog settings.

Next, let's drill down yet again and use this tool on a data sub-subsample; that is, on just a small portion of a data sample, such as the first part of the word "audio" that you did surgery on in Chapter 7.

Partial Subsample Analysis: Smaller Selections

Select the first portion of the vocal "audio" word sample (see Figure 9-13), and again, invoke **Analyze ➤ Plot Spectrum** to analyze this snippet (or sub-subsample).

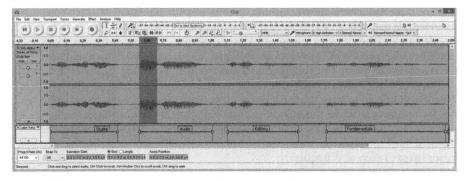

Figure 9-13. *Select an even smaller snippet on front of "audio"*

As shown in the left-hand screenshot in Figure 9-14, you can see the frequency data even more clearly. The fewer data samples that you select, the more clearly you can see the frequency distribution. This is because the data has more room to spread out inside the Frequency Analysis window, as is evident on both sides of Figure 9-14. Notice that in the right-hand screenshot, I changed the **Algorithm** from Spectrum to Standard Autocorrelation.

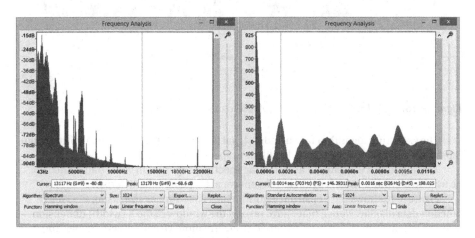

Figure 9-14. *Spectral analysis of first portion of word "audio"*

In case you are wondering what these three different algorithm types do, the **Spectrum** algorithm, which is a default setting, plots the FFT of your audio spectrum data. FFT stands for **Fast Fourier Transform**; it is the algorithm that computes the **Discrete Fourier Transform** (DFT) of any data sequence.

Fast Fourier analysis converts the signal (audio sample data) from its original mathematical domain, usually over time, to a spatial representation; in this case of digital audio waveforms, it is both. This allows you to visualize your data in a different way, which can be quite helpful in assisting you in your workflow decision-making process.

73

The three **Autocorrelation** algorithm options measure the extent to which your audio sample data repeats itself. This algorithm does this by taking two copies of the sample data and then moving one forward by one sample. These two copies are then multiplied together and all the values are summed. This is repeated for two samples difference, and so on, up to a number of samples that you specify using the size option.

Autocorrelation gives a small result if the waveform is random (such as white, pink, or Brownian noise), and a large result if it is repetitive (like a decaying, held, musical note).

By looking at peaks for this algorithm's data plot, your key frequencies can still be determined, even if there's a lot of noise in the data sample. Figure 9-15 shows the Standard Autocorrelation algorithm using 2048 and 4096 data sample sizes. Note that the cursor snaps to each peak frequency.

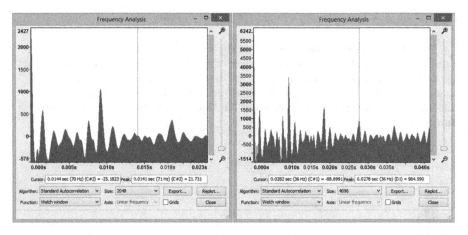

Figure 9-15. *A Welch function at 2048 or 4096 can simulate waves*

The Cepstrum algorithm for an audio signal is related to the Spectrum algorithm, but represents a rate of change across the different spectrum bands.

This algorithm is useful for ascertaining spectral properties in vocal tracks and can be used to identify speakers by their different vocal frequency characteristics!

Figure 9-16 shows the Cepstrum algorithm at a 256 samples size, using the Welch function data display. Notice that I have resized the window in the X (width) dimension to space out these data curves so that their peaks are more visually ascertainable. You should leverage this feature because you can also resize this window in the Y (height) dimension if you need to fit a different spectral data graphing view. All in all, the Frequency Analysis dialog is a very powerful data visualization tool.

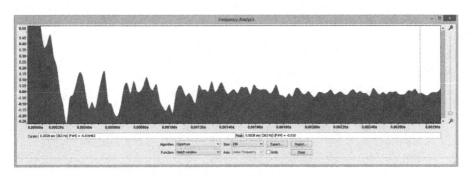

Figure 9-16. *A Cepstrum algorithm, at 256 frequency sample size*

Be sure to experiment with all the different settings and features that this Plot Spectrum tool can provide for your digital audio editing.

Summary

In this chapter, you explored the Analyze menu and various algorithmic analysis tools, including the visual analysis of frequency spectrums using the Plot Spectrum tool, and tools that create Label Track data and export sample analysis data in numeric format. You looked at how to analyze progressively smaller data samples to drill down into visual analytical data representations. And you looked at the three different algorithm categories that you can use to analyze your data.

In the next chapter, you learn all about **digital audio data compositing** concepts and principles via Audacity's **Tracks** menu.

CHAPTER 10

■ ■ ■

The Compositing of Digital Audio: Using Tracks

You now have an understanding of how to use algorithmic tools in Audacity to not only process your audio sample data for what it sounds like, but also for visual analysis. Now it's time to go back to what I call "manual editing tools," given that the algorithms do the work for you once you direct them with a setting or two (or sometimes half a dozen). In this chapter, you will look at the concept of tracks, accessed using the **Tracks** menu in Audacity. You encountered the Label Track in Chapter 9, and you go over the other track types in this chapter.

Tracks in digital audio editing software provide similar functionality to layers in digital image compositing software, as they allow you to separate content (or features) into their own containers for more content editing workflow flexibility.

Layers in digital image compositing software allow you to create image composites. Similarly, tracks in audio software allow you to create **digital audio composites**.

You'll finish looking at the **Label Tracks** features first, move on to Time Tracks, and then look at related features such as **envelopes** before you get into Stereo Tracks and **Mono Tracks**. You'll discover how to work with tracks, from basics such as resizing to more advanced "moves" such as turning Stereo Tracks into Mono Tracks.

Audio Compositing and Utility Tracks

By adding either Stereo or Mono Tracks to your project, you can "composite," or layer, digital audio assets together to create complex audio assets. For instance, you can add background music or sound effects and mix them in with your vocal tracks. There's also what I call "utility" tracks, which allow you to add things like **selection sets**, **labels**, and **envelopes** to your Audacity project. These features are in Audacity's Tracks menu.

Label Tracks: Text Label Subsample Selection

You already got a head start in Chapter 9, when you used the Analyze menu's Regular Interval Labels function (see Figure 9-1) to create a **Label Track**. Let's finish learning about this Label Track type by taking a look at the **Tracks ➤ Edit Labels** menu sequence,

---

Electronic supplementary material The online version of this chapter (doi:10.1007/978-1-4842-1648-4_10) contains supplementary material, which is available to authorized users.

© Wallace Jackson 2015
W. Jackson, *Digital Audio Editing Fundamentals*, DOI 10.1007/978-1-4842-1648-4_10

which opens the Edit Labels dialog and allows you to do all the Label Track label editing in one central location. As you can see in Figure 10-1, there's an extra **vocal** label, which is shown highlighted in the lower-right corner of Audacity. Click the **5** in the dialog, which selects this unused label entry, and click the **Remove** button to delete it from the Label Track view pane.

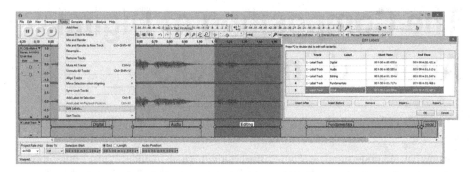

Figure 10-1. *Use the Edit labels dialog and delete vocal label*

As you can see in Figure 10-2, the vocal label is gone. Also shown in Figures 10-1 and 10-2 is that if you click a label name, Audacity selects that label's range (which I call a "selection set") if you have set the label range using dots and arrowheads, as you learned in Chapter 9.

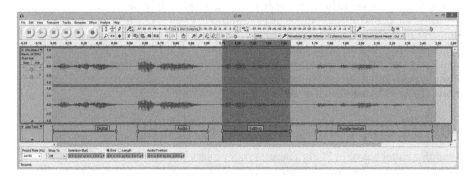

Figure 10-2. *Label can also be used for subsample selection set*

Thus, you can use Label Tracks to define **selection sets**.

Time Tracks: Project Time or Rate (Pitch) Warping

Let's look at another utility (tool) track in Audacity called a **Time Track**. Whereas the Label Track is logically at the bottom of your project, as shown in Figure 10-3, the Time Track should logically be placed at the top of the project. To create a Time Track, use the **Tracks ► Add New ► Time Track** menu sequence. Audacity automatically positions your Time Track at the top of the Audacity project.

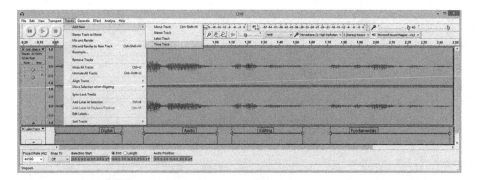

Figure 10-3. Use Tracks menu and Add New ➤ Time Track submenu

As you can see in Figure 10-4, the new Time Track, which is labeled at the left side of the track (as are the Stereo Track and the Label Track), is now at the top of your Audacity project.

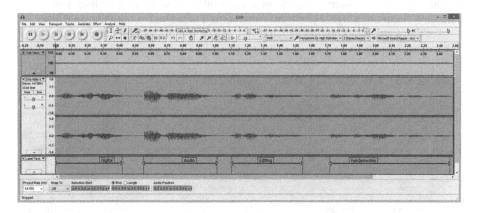

Figure 10-4. A Time Track is added to the top of your project

Anything that you do in this Time Track affects your entire project, just like the Label Track. You can close a track at any time by clicking the **X** in the upper-left corner of the track. Click in the **gray area** at the left to select that track.

Resizing and Using a Time Track: Add a Pitch Shifting Envelope

To resize the Time Track, place your cursor on top of the line that divides the area between your Time Track and Stereo Track, until the cursor turns into a **double-headed arrow**, and then click and drag downward. To affect the **Time Track control data**, which is shown as a blue line in Figure 10-4, you use the **Envelope Tool**, which is shown circled in red in Figure 10-5.

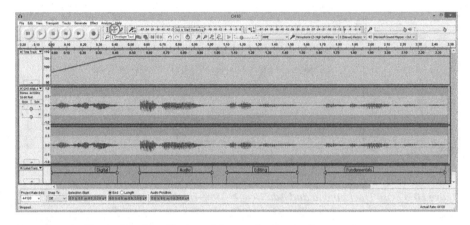

Figure 10-5. *Use the Envelope Tool to add control points to line*

Click to insert a **control point** on your left end of the Timeline, and then one at 0.40, and then drag the left control point down to a level of 97, as seen in Figure 10-5. This starts your sample at a higher pitch and then ramps it to normal, using a diagonal line.

Let's do something complex with the tool, and chipmunk some of these samples, as is shown in Figure 10-6.

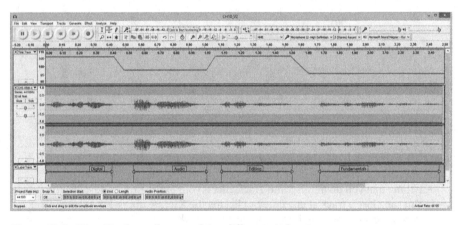

Figure 10-6. *Time Track envelope applying different pitch rates*

As you can see in Figure 10-6, I added control points so that I could increase the playback rate (pitch), for some of the subsamples. I changed this rate during the periods of silence in between the subsamples, and then decreased the playback rate, which I did twice, using different pitch (rates) for each subsample. You can clearly see what I did by using the Envelope Tool in the Time Track. And now if you play the project, each subsample uses a different pitch.

You can also use the Envelope Tool in the Stereo or Mono Tracks; however, in these tracks, it affects the amplitude, not the frequency of the waveform! Let's look at that next.

Using Other Track Envelopes: Control Amplitude, Not Frequency

As you can see in **Stereo Tracks**, you have the same control data ribbon, or spline, that you have in your Time Track. These blue lines appear whenever you select the Envelope Tool. You can manipulate them in the same way that you do in the Time Track: using control points that can be entered by clicking the line, or anywhere in the Track for that matter. In the Mono and Stereo Tracks, these control data lines control amplitude, so if you wanted to peak the volume for each of your subsample portions in your voice-over, it would look something like what's shown in Figure 10-7.

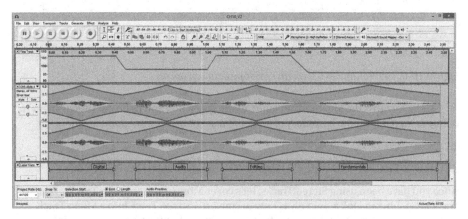

Figure 10-7. *Using Envelopes for Stereo Track to control volume*

Next, let's implement a different envelope configuration to provide the same effect that the Silence Audio Tool or Noise Reduction algorithm accomplished previously.

There are different approaches to achieving the same result using professional new-media content-production software packages. This is a third way to silence noise by using amplitude.

Using the amplitude envelope to turn down the volume between data samples effectively does the same thing that the tool-based and algorithm-based approaches did, so you can reduce noise by using an envelope, an algorithm, or a tool. Not bad for a fundamentals book, eh?

In Figure 10-8, you can see that I've aligned these envelopes, as well as the labels, across all four tracks. Also, notice in Figures 10-7 and 10-8 that if you put the cursor in the top time indicator bar (above all the tracks), it turns into a down arrow that indicates where you are in the project; the line attached to it is either white (see Figure 10-7) or yellow (see Figure 10-8).

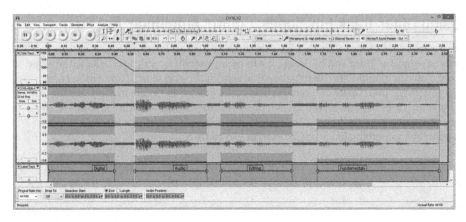

Figure 10-8. *Set Volume to 0 with an envelope between vocals*

Audacity turns the line that's attached to the green position indicator (down arrow) a yellow color if it is on the boundary of a selection set or in a control point position.

Mono Tracks: Some Audio Doesn't Require Stereo

Since you have been using Stereo Tracks, let's cover Monoaural, or **Mono Tracks**, first. The logical thing to look at initially is how to convert a Stereo Track into a Mono Track. The reason you want to do this is two-fold. First, although this isn't a data footprint optimization chapter, having to compress, optimize, and store half of a data sample means a 100% reduction in any resulting file size, using any of the digital audio formats covered in Chapter 4. This savings simply can't be ignored. The moral of the story is don't use Stereo Tracks unless you absolutely have to for digital audio asset quality. The other reason is because Stereo Tracks are not really needed for things such as sound effects.

Stereo Track to Mono Track: Conversion Algorithm

To convert a Stereo Track to a Mono Track, click in the blank gray area at the far left of the Stereo track under the track settings. This selects your entire track, as shown in Figure 10-9. Notice that Audacity is now showing the Label Track selection set areas that you defined in the previous two chapters. Audacity is smart, as long as you set up the project correctly, which I have been showing you how to do.

Now you are ready to combine these Stereo Tracks into one Mono Track. To do this, select **Tracks ➤ Stereo Track to Mono**, as shown in Figure 10-9.

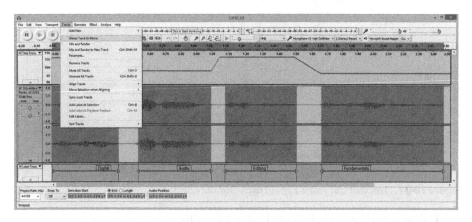

Figure 10-9. *Select Tracks ➤ Stereo Track to Mono*

Your stereo voice-over sample data is now mono voice-over sample data contained in a Mono Track, as shown in Figure 10-10. Notice that this track sounds essentially the same if you play it back.

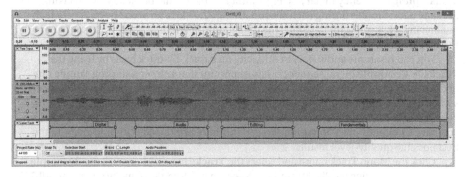

Figure 10-10. *Mono Track is the summary of Stereo Track data*

If you click the left side of the Mono track, next to its track name area, your entire Mono Track should be selected. However, your selection sets are not individually shown as they were before, thus something has changed during this transition. Let's investigate this further to see which of the selection sets, labels, or envelopes (volume) control data might have disappeared.

As you can see in Figure 10-11, your Label Track data is still intact, and if you click the label names in the selection set, the data is also still in place. However, if you click the Envelope Tool icon (shown selected in Figure 10-11), you'll find that the envelope data was lost in the algorithmic combination of the tracks.

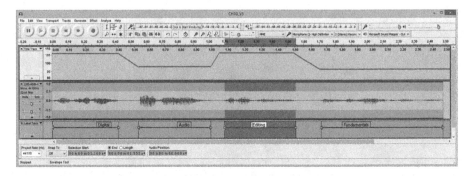

Figure 10-11. *You can still select Label Track, but the envelopes are gone*

Let's hope that the Audacity Team is working on this!

Let's take a look at some of the other important editing functions in the Tracks menu.

Track Resampling: Changing the Track Sampling Frequency

The other significant way to reduce the data footprint in your digital audio assets is to cut the **sampling frequency** in half, saving another 100% in data, because you are taking half as many data samples during each second. Using 22.05 kHz for voice-overs is very high quality; in fact, if you want to reduce the data footprint another 200%, you could resample to 11.25 kHz and still get a good voice-over reproduction.

You can resample audio data in Audacity on a track-by-track basis by using the **Tracks ➤ Resample** menu sequence. It is important that you set a starting sample rate of CD quality (44.1 kHz), or even THX quality (48 kHz), so that later you have plenty of source data for your resampling algorithm to work with. It also helps to resample to an even multiple of 2, 4, or 8, if possible. In this case, $4 \times 11.25 = 44.1$ and $2 \times 22.05 = 44.1$, so you have a perfectly even downsample scenario, allowing the algorithm to give you the best possible quality-level results.

Click the Mono Track name and select the **Tracks** menu. Then click the **Resample** menu option, selecting the 22050 sampling rate from the drop-down menu (see Figure 10-12). Click the **OK** button to resample the Mono Track at 22.05 kHz.

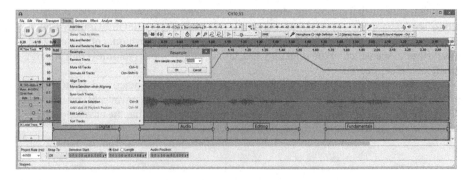

Figure 10-12. *Set new sample frequency using Tracks ➤ Resample*

Next, let's take a quick look at the **Sort Tracks** feature.

Tracks Reordering: Using the Sort Tracks Submenu

By selecting **Tracks ➤ Sort Tracks** (see Figure 10-13), Audacity allows you to sort your tracks at any time, either by a data sample's start time, which you would use if you had these four subsamples on their own tracks, or by Track Name. It doesn't matter which tracks are selected because it sorts the tracks across your entire project. Let's use the **Sort Tracks by Name** option to see how this function works on your current project. This gives you a new perspective of looking at your digital audio sample data, time warp (pitch rate) control data, and label data.

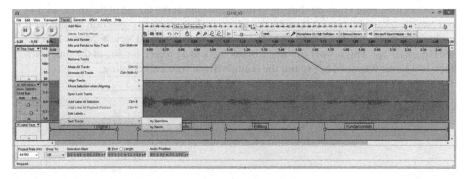

Figure 10-13. *Use the Tracks ➤ Sort Tracks ➤ by Name function*

As you can see in Figure 10-14, the current tracks have been sorted into a different order, with the sample waveform on top, the label selection sets underneath that, and the envelope control data underneath that. In this configuration, you can see that the control point relationship to the selection sets better, so I refined these even more using the track configuration; now the points and selection set lines align even better than before.

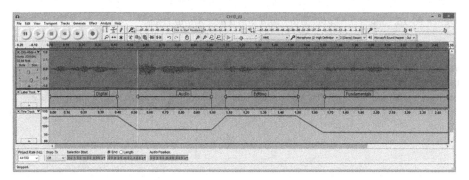

Figure 10-14. *Your tracks are now rearranged by track name*

Now let's return to the Stereo project version by using the **Edit ➤ Undo** menu sequence several times. Alternatively, you could simply open your **CH10_V3.aud** project.

It is important to note that Audacity 2.1 uses an **undo queue**, which keeps track of your "moves" and can undo whatever you have done as far back as you need to undo it, which can be quite handy. This is a feature in production software packages such as GIMP, Blender, Lightworks, and Inkscape, among others. These are all covered in my *Android Studio New Media Fundamentals* (Apress, 2015) title.

Next, let's look at adding a new blank track and placing synthesized tone data into it. I'll cover synthesis in Audacity, which is found in the **Generate** menu, in the next chapter.

Adding Tracks: Creating a New Track

First, select the Label Track by clicking in the blank area at the far left of the track, so that your New Track is underneath it, since the labels are being used as selection set guides for the Stereo track above the Label Track. Then select **Tracks ➤ Add New ➤ Mono Track** (see Figure 10-15). This is how you add a blank track to a project, for any of the four track types, whenever you need to expand the complexity of your compositing.

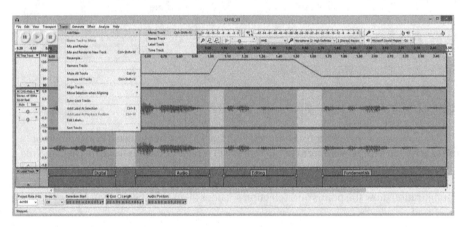

Figure 10-15. *Select the Label Track and add a new Mono Track*

As you can see in Figure 10-16, the blank track is added underneath the Label Track. You can use the **Generate ➤ DTMF Tones** menu sequence to synthesize audio in this new track. I named the DTMF sequence **telephonedialer**, used 50% volume to composite the audio with the voice-overs, and used a one-half second duration with a sample rate duration setting of 22050 Hz. The resulting tones are seen in Figure 10-17.

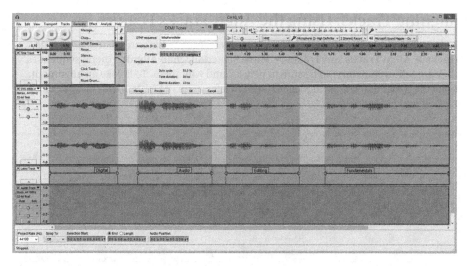

Figure 10-16. *A Mono Track will be added under your Label Track*

Next, let's look at how to reposition tracks so that the tone sequence aligns before the vocals start.

Dragging Tracks: Repositioning Your Track Order

You need to position the Mono Track before the Stereo Track in the audio composite. This is done using a drag-and-drop operation, as shown in Figure 10-17 ("before" the drag-and-drop is shown in the left screen; "after" is shown in the right screen).

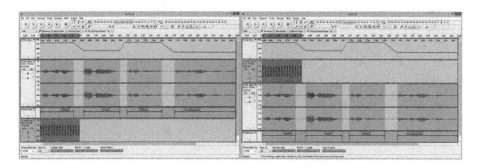

Figure 10-17. *Drag the Mono Audio Track above your Stereo Track*

To reposition tracks in this manner, you click the track name and information area, and drag the track up or down to reposition it. Now that your tracks are in the right order for using track alignment features, let's take a look at that next.

Aligning Tracks: Using the Align Tracks Feature

Audacity has a number of useful track alignment features, which are located under the **Tracks ➤ Align Tracks** and **Tracks ➤ Move Selection when Aligning** menu sequences. They are self-explanatory, so be sure to play around with them. To invoke an alignment, select the tracks that you want to align (see the left screen in Figure 10-18) and select a track alignment option.

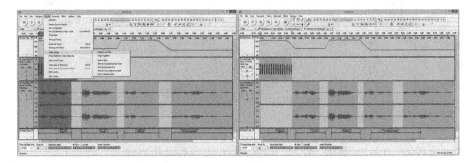

Figure 10-18. *Shift-select multiple tracks, and use Track Align*

As you can see in the right-hand screen in Figure 10-18, the **Align End to End** function aligns the audio compositing project so that your Mono Track DTMF Tones plays back before any of your vocal samples are played.

Take a close look at the bottom of the right screen in Figure 10-18; a problem was introduced with the alignment of the Label Track. You need to drag the right (or left) dot for each of the selection set labels, and reposition them back underneath the subsamples in the Stereo Track. This lets you be more proactive with Audacity, so it's a good thing.

To add a selection set label for the DTMF Tone Sequence, you want to use the selection (vertical bar) tool and then select the area of space where you want the selection set range to be defined, as shown at the bottom of Figure 10-19.

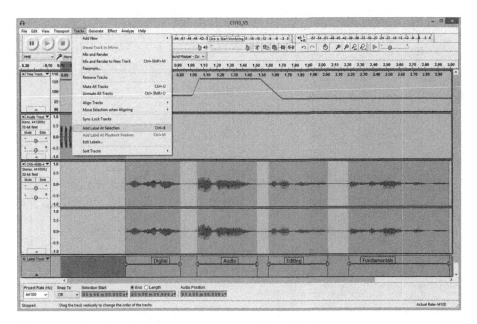

Figure 10-19. *Align selection set labels, and select left area*

Next, select **Tracks ➤ Add Label At Selection** (see Figure 10-19). This tells Audacity to create the selection set label range and sets the dots and chevrons!

As you can see on the bottom-left of Figure 10-20, all that you have to do is type the **DTMF Tone Sequence** label, and the Label Track is upgraded to contain your selection set for the DTMF Tone section that was added. You're done once you adjust the envelope data.

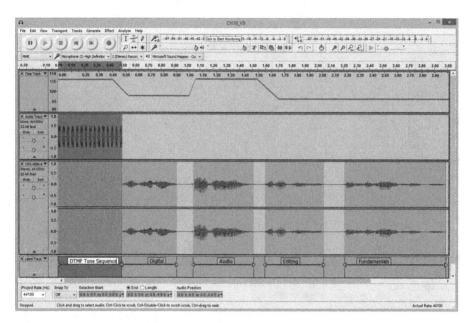

Figure 10-20. *Edit a text field for the new selection set label*

You may have also noticed in Figure 10-20 that the data for the envelope control points has not been shifted over with the align tool, so you have to get some more practice with Audacity and move them 0.5 seconds to the right for each of the control points.

Once you have done this, your Audacity project should look like the one shown in Figure 10-21. I saved the project as CH10_V6.aud so that you have it in the book repository.

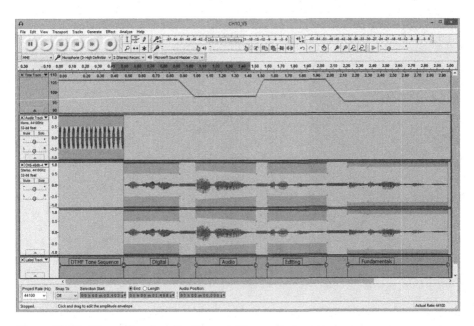

Figure 10-21. *Use an Envelope Tool to reposition control points*

Make sure to get a good amount of practice with the tool collection on the Tracks menu, as tracks are the main way to separate your editing moves and sample data for your Audacity 2.1 projects.

Using all the tools that you've learned about thus far, such as envelopes, selection sets, algorithms, and so on, you should be able to assemble any audio composite that you'll need for your multimedia production and digital audio asset creation process.

Summary

In this chapter, you looked at how to create digital audio compositing projects by using the tracks features found in Audacity 2.1. You looked more closely at Label Tracks, added a Time Track, and converted a Stereo Track to a Mono Track. You added a new track with synthesized dial tones. You also learned how to manipulate tracks in different ways and how to align tracks to each other.

In the next chapter, you learn about **digital audio synthesis** tools in the **Generate** menu in Audacity 2.1.

CHAPTER 11

■ ■ ■

The Synthesis of Digital Audio: Tone Generation

Now that you have learned how to composite digital audio tracks using Audacity's Tracks menu, you should also take a look at the Generate menu, which allows you to synthesize digital audio using algorithms ranging from chirps and tones, to different types of noise, or even silence. There are even Generate menu plug-ins preinstalled in Audacity for metronome click tracks, plucked strings, and Risset Drum instruments. You already looked at the synthesis algorithm that generates DTMF Tones, so Audacity is fairly adept at synthesizing audio.

You will look at how to synthesize digital audio samples from scratch using these algorithms, as well as how to find, download, and install third-party generator algorithms to "buff out" your Audacity 2.1 Generator menu, which I'm sure you will want to do. In fact, let's get greedy and do that first!

Installing Nyquist Generate Menu Plug-Ins

Before you learn to use all of these different audio synthesis tone generators in Audacity's Generate menu, let's go to the **Audacity Team Wiki** and download seven of the coolest tone generation plug-ins so that you have enhanced the synthesis capabilities of Audacity 2.1 installation by about 100%. These are located on the **Nyquist Generate Plug-Ins** page at http://wiki.audacityteam.org/wiki/Nyquist_Generate_Plug-ins.

If you scroll down this web page (see Figure 11-1), you'll find a number of different Audacity Generate menu plug-ins that are free to download and install. This is exactly what you're going to do to get all of these cool synths!

© Wallace Jackson 2015
W. Jackson, *Digital Audio Editing Fundamentals*, DOI 10.1007/978-1-4842-1648-4_11

Figure 11-1. *Audacity Nyquist Generate Plugins download page*

As you download each plug-in ZIP file, extract it to the Nyquest_Generate_Plug-Ins folder on your hard disk drive. Next, copy the **.ny** files to your **\Audacity\Plug-Ins** folder, as shown in Figure 11-2. I'm using Windows 8, so mine is in C:\Program Files(x86)\ Audacity\Plug-Ins\.

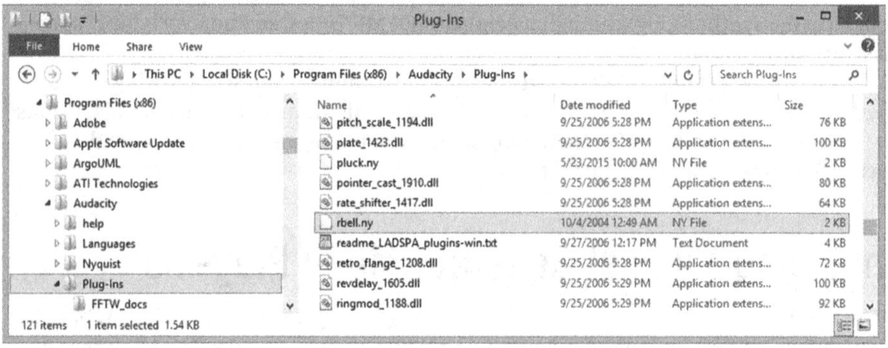

Figure 11-2. *The C:\ProgramFiles(x86)\Audacity\Plug-Ins folder*

Let's download and install seven plug-ins: Risset Bell (to go with the Risset Drum already in Audacity), the Explosion effect generator, KLSTRBAS, Tuning Fork (to go with the Metronome Click Generator), Oxygene Surf Generator, Harmonic Noise engine, and PWM (pulse-wave modulation).

Once these have been decompressed (unzipped), and copied into your Plug-Ins folder, launch Audacity, which finds the new Nyquist Audio Generator Plug-Ins and adds them to the Manage menu option in the Effect and Analyze menus, as well as the Generate menu.

Any menu that allows you to add a third-party algorithm features the **Manage** menu option. All three menus access the **Plug-in Manager: Effects, Generators and Analyzers** dialog, which is shown in Figure 11-3.

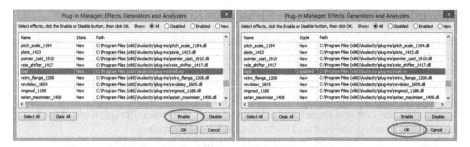

Figure 11-3. Plug-in Manager: Effects, Generators and Analyzers

Find the Risset Bell plug-in that you just decompressed and copied. Select it (see the left screen in Figure 11-3) and click **Enable** so that it shows in your Generate menu (as seen in the right screen in Figure 11-3). Click the **OK** button and close the dialog.

When you look at the Generate menu, Risset Bell is now right next to Risset Drum; these two siblings are reunited in sonic harmony forever. This is shown highlighted in Figure 11-4 in the left of the screen. Generate plug-ins that are DLLs and come with Audacity appear at the top of the menu and Nyquist tone generators are on the bottom.

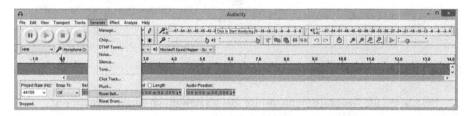

Figure 11-4. Risset Bell Generator is now on your Generate menu

Now you're ready to look at more than a half dozen of the 15 audio synthesis plug-ins installed on the Generate menu. If you plan to use Audacity for digital audio synthesis, there are many more of these plug-ins—so see if you can make your Generate menu as long as the Effect menu! You can also install third-party spectral analysis tools if you are into visual analysis (covered in Chapter 9).

Audacity Synthesizer: The Generate Menu

For the duration of this chapter, let's get some practice using these useful and impressive Nyquist digital audio synthesizer plug-ins. You'll look at how to create a new empty Stereo Track, how to use seven of the audio synthesis options, and see what these synthesized waveforms look like. I find this area of Audacity and digital audio editing a lot of fun, so I hope that you find it the same.

Virtual Surf Waveforms: Oxygene Surf Generator

The first thing that you need to do is create a Stereo Track so that there is somewhere for the synthesized audio to live. I normally use a Mono Track for sound effects, such as the Fire and Explosion generator, but some of these effects require a Stereo Track, such as the Oxygene Wave generator. All of them utilize a Stereo Track if it is present; I opted to use a Stereo Track so that you can see the Generate plug-ins that support it. If a Stereo Track is supported, the Left and Right Channel data samples will look different; if only Mono Tracks are supported, the Left and Right Channel data is identical.

Launch Audacity 2.1 and use the **Tracks ➤ Add New ➤ Stereo Channel** menu sequence to add an empty Stereo Track to your new digital audio synthesis project (see Figure 11-5).

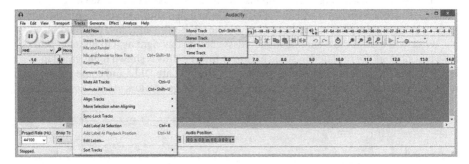

Figure 11-5. *Add a track using Tracks ➤ Add New ➤ Stereo Track*

Next, select the **Generate** menu. Notice that it's now much longer because you doubled the number of tone generator synthesizers.

Let's start with a more relaxing Generate menu synthesizer—the David R. Sky Oxygene Surf generator. If you like Surf generators, there is also the **LFO Surf** generator by David R. Sky, which is more generic (no pun intended).

Select the **Generate** menu and the **Surf [Oxygene]** option, which opens the Surf [Oxygene] dialog (see Figure 11-6).

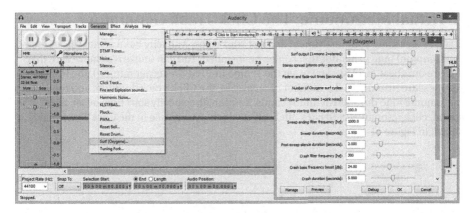

Figure 11-6. *Select the Generate ➤ Surf [Oxygene] menu sequence*

I used the stereo **Surf output** option, with an 80% spread, 0 fade effect, 10 cycles, pink noise generation, 100 Hz start frequency and 1000 Hz ending frequency, 1.5 second sweep duration, 2 seconds of post-sweep silence, a 300 Hz **Crash filter frequency**, 24 decibels of **Crash bass frequency boost**, and a **Crash duration** of 5 seconds.

As you can see in Figure 11-7, the Oxygene Wave waveform synthesis signature is very unique and different across the two channels. Use the **play** button to preview crashing ocean waves!

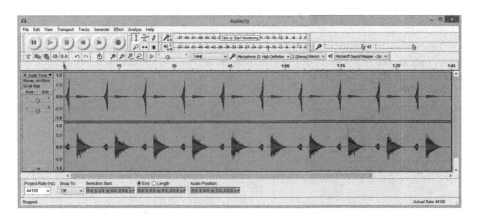

Figure 11-7. *Preview the Oxygene Wave Stereo Track audio sample*

Next, let's take a look at a more useful tone generator, **Click Track**, the virtual metronome for Audacity.

97

A Virtual Metronome: The Click Track Generator

If you're recording your instrument and not your voice, Audacity has a useful Click Track (metronome) tone generator that comes preinstalled. You can utilize it to make sure that you are on a beat. It allows you to set the Tempo in BPM (beats per minute), the beats per measure (usually 4), the number of measures, the Click Track duration, and the metronome tone duration in milliseconds. You can also specify start time offset, click sound, click resonance, and click pitch, all of which you can see in the Click Track dialog shown in Figure 11-8.

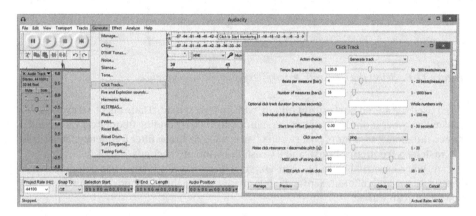

Figure 11-8. *Select the Generate ➤ Click Track menu sequence*

I accepted the default setting values and clicked the **OK** button to generate the Stereo Click Track shown in Figure 11-9. Click the **play** button to preview the metronome click track now.

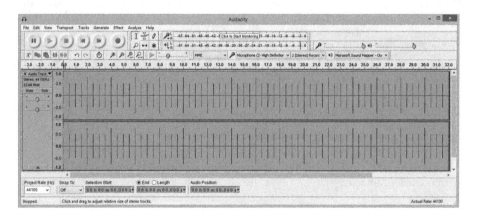

Figure 11-9. *Preview the Stereo Click Track audio data sample*

It's important to note that you can use a Mono Track for this metronome click-track functionality. So if you're going to use it when recording instrument performances, use the **Tracks ➤ Add New ➤ Mono Track** menu sequence, rather than using a Stereo Track, although that works as well.

Next, let's look at another useful tone generator, David R. Sky's **Tuning Fork** generator, the virtual tuning fork in Audacity.

A Virtual Tuning Fork: The Tuning Fork Generator

Before you start recording instrumental music tracks in Audacity, you should use the Tuning Fork generator to make sure that your instruments are in tune. This tone generator allows you to set the **Tone duration**, which I set to 1.0 second; **Constant volume or a fade out**, which I selected to simulate a real-world tuning fork; and **MIDI note** or (optional) **frequency**. I used the default MIDI note of 69, as you can see in the Tuning Fork dialog in Figure 11-10. If you want to use a C note (music, not money) for a tuning fork, use a MIDI note value of 60.

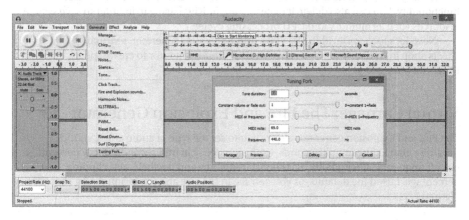

Figure 11-10. *Select the Generate ➤ Tuning Fork menu sequence*

I accepted the default values and clicked the **OK** button to generate the Tuning Fork track shown in Figure 11-11. Click the **play** button to preview your tuning fork tone now.

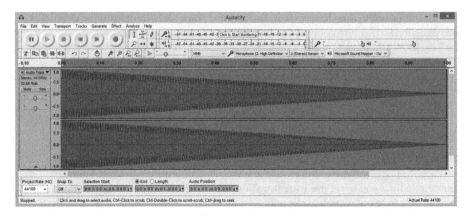

Figure 11-11. *Preview the Stereo Tuning Fork audio data sample*

It's important to note that you can use a Mono Track for this tuning fork track functionality. You can also delete it once you are finished using it, in order to save system resources such as memory and CPU processing cycles.

Next, let's look at David R. Sky's **Fire and Explosion** generator, a virtual special effects shop in Audacity 2.1! You can use this FX tone generator to create special audio effects for your games.

Virtual Carnage: The Fire and Explosion Generator

The Fire and Explosion generator allows you to set the type of audio effect, sound duration, attack time in milliseconds, explosion decay in milliseconds, decay percentage, cut-off frequency, filter quality, Bass boost frequency and decibels, and clipping percentage. I used the defaults, as you can see in the Fire and Explosion dialog shown in Figure 11-12.

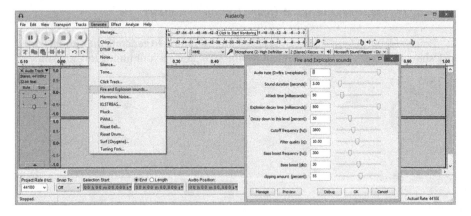

Figure 11-12. *Select your Generate ➤ Fire and Explosion sounds*

I accepted the default setting values and clicked the **OK** button to generate the Explosion effect track (see Figure 11-13). Click the **play** button to preview the explosion effect.

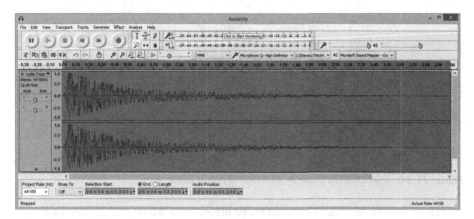

Figure 11-13. *Preview the Stereo explosion audio data sample*

Next, let's look at Steven Jones' **KLSTRBAS** generator, which stands for **cluster bass**.

Virtual Cluster Bass: The KLSTRBAS Generator

According to KLSTRBAS tone generator author, Steve Jones: "KLSTRBAS generates dense sounds by combining several waveforms with a fixed frequency ratio between them. Early Roland drum machines created cymbal sound in part by combining multiple square waves with non-integral frequency ratios. The combined signal was then high-pass filtered to produce a very dense cluster of high frequency harmonics. The genesis of KLSTRBAS was a failed attempt to create cymbal sounds using this technique."

As you can see in Figure 11-14, the KLSTRBAS dialog allows you to set your **MIDI key** (note value), **Decay** value, **Fractional Decay** value, **Density** value, **Detune** value, **Flange** value, and **Wave table** indicator value.

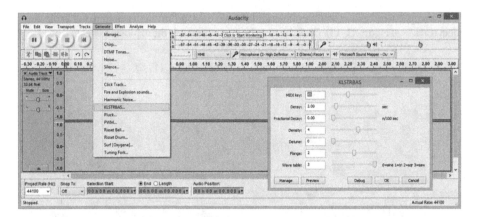

Figure 11-14. *Select the Generate ➤ KLSTRBAS menu sequence*

The wave table indicator can be set to one of four value settings: 0 indicates a sine wave table, 1 indicates a triangle wave table, 2 indicates a square wave table, and 3 indicates a saw wave table.

As evident in the KLSTRBAS dialog, you have a great deal of variation in creating cool tones with this generator. I set the A3 note is the MIDI key, a 2-second decay, a fractional decay value of 0, a density value of 4, a detune value of 0, and a middle flange value of 2. I use the square (also called a pulse) wave table by specifying a value of 3.

I accepted the default setting values and clicked the **OK** button to generate the Cluster Bass data track (see Figure 11-15). Click the **play** button to preview the sample.

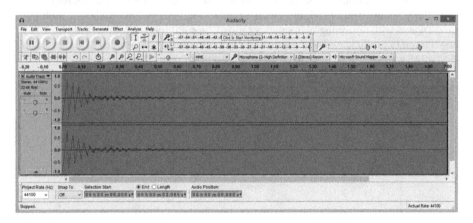

Figure 11-15. *Preview the Stereo Cluster Bass audio data sample*

Next, let's take a look at the harmonic noise generator.

Extraterrestrial Vocals: Harmonic Noise Generator

The harmonic noise generator allows you to set a **MIDI Note List** and the **Number of Harmonics** to generate from this list. There are also **Duration**, **Band Width**, and **Odd Harmonics Only** options in the Harmonic Noise dialog (see Figure 11-16) to generate a very unique noise track.

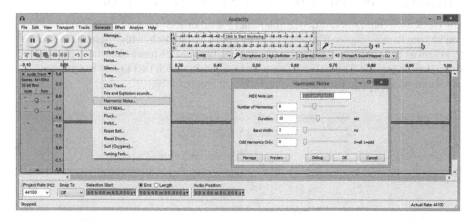

Figure 11-16. *Select a Generate* ➤ *Harmonic Noise menu sequence*

I accepted the default setting values and clicked the **OK** button, generating the Harmonic Noise sample data track seen in Figure 11-17. Click the **play** button to preview the Harmonic Noise stereo sample, which you'll see (and hear) is out-of-this-world extraterrestrial in nature. The waveforms even look like alien centipedes—and they sound even stranger than they look!

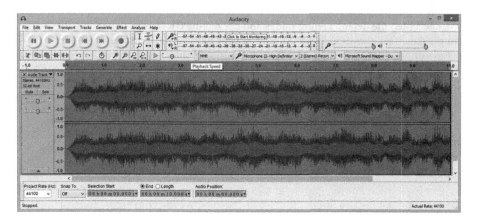

Figure 11-17. *Preview the Stereo Harmonic Noise audio sample*

Next, let's return to an audio tone generator that comes preinstalled in Audacity 2.1—the **Pluck** tone generator. No, not the Cluster Pluck generator; let's keep it clean here. It's just a simple pluck-string instrument generator that can be used to simulate bass guitars, guitars, or even banjos, using the proper digital audio effects processing.

Virtual String Instrument: The Pluck Generator

The Pluck tone generator is much simpler than the other audio synthesis algorithms you've seen in this chapter. It allows you to set **Pluck MIDI Pitch**, which defaults to middle C, as well as **Fade-out type**, which I set to gradual, because it's more like what a plucked string does in real life. There is also Duration in seconds, which I set to 1.00 second. You can see these options in the Pluck dialog shown in Figure 11-18.

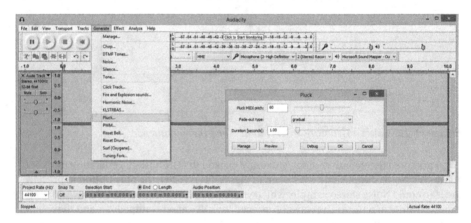

Figure 11-18. *Select the Generate ➤ Pluck menu sequence*

I accepted the default setting values and clicked the **OK** button, generating the Pluck sample data track shown in Figure 11-19. Click the **play** button to preview the Pluck stereo sample. I noticed a high level at the beginning of the sample, so I took a screenshot of the playback to show this.

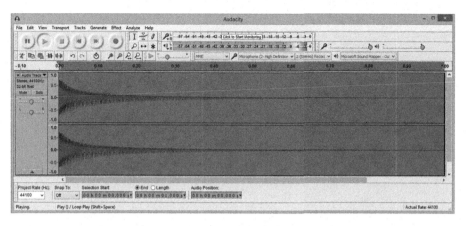

Figure 11-19. *Preview a Stereo Pluck digital audio data sample*

This is most likely because a plucked string generates a high decibel level right after the string is released, generating all of its audio "power," or its amplitude, at that initial point in time.

These Generate menu digital audio synthesizers, or waveform generation algorithms, bring a lot of power to your digital audio editing and compositing work process.

If you think "outside of the box" and utilize Audacity's vast Effect menu in conjunction with the Analyze menu, you will be able to create any digital audio assets that you need for your multimedia projects.

Summary

In this chapter, you looked at digital audio synthesis, known as **tone generation** in Audacity, using the Generator menu. First, you doubled the amount of tone generation algorithms in Audacity 2.1.1, and then you learned how and where to get even more of these Nyquist plug-ins.

After that, you looked at seven of the most useful tone generator algorithms available to Audacity. You explored their algorithm configuration dialogs and the resulting synthesized digital audio waveforms.

In the next chapter, you learn about **digital audio data footprint optimization** concepts, terms, and principles.

CHAPTER 12

■ ■ ■

The Data Footprint of Digital Audio: Compression

You now know the fundamental concepts, terminology, principles, and work processes surrounding digital audio editing, compositing, and synthesis, which allows you to create digital audio assets for your new media content. Now it is time to get into digital audio **data footprint optimization** and the way to go about getting the smallest possible digital audio file size for your audio assets, while at the same time getting the pristine audio playback quality results that you need for your interactive digital application development.

You'll look at the primary considerations for optimizing your digital audio asset, including **device compatibility** (a baseline digital audio asset to gauge compression against each codec that you learned about in Chapter 4), optimizing digital audio usage (system memory and in network bandwidth considerations), and similar advanced topics on how digital audio is used.

Audio Optimization: Device Compatibility

Optimizing your digital audio assets for playback across the widest range of platforms, operating systems, and hardware devices is going to be easier than optimizing digital video or digital image assets. This is because there's a wide range of display screen resolutions and aspect ratios compared to the more limited range of digital audio playback support (except for the latest Android hardware featuring 24-bit HD Audio playback compatibility).

People's ears can't perceive the same quality differences in digital audio that their eyes can perceive in digital images. There are two important "sweet spots" for digital audio support across hardware devices that you should target. A lower-quality audio (narration track or sound effects) use an 8 kHz or an 11.25 kHz sampling rate, with 8-bit, 12-bit, or 16-bit sample resolution.

Medium-quality audio (game music loops, longer sound effects, ambient background audio) use a 22.05 kHz or a 32 kHz sampling rate, with 12-bit or 16-bit sample resolution.

Electronic supplementary material The online version of this chapter (doi:10.1007/978-1-4842-1648-4_12) contains supplementary material, which is available to authorized users.

W. Jackson, *Digital Audio Editing Fundamentals*, DOI 10.1007/978-1-4842-1648-4_12

High-quality audio (albums, music for listening, film scores, etc.), including CD quality and HD quality audio, use 16-bit (CD quality) or 24-bit (HD quality) sample resolution at a 44.1 kHz or a 48 kHz sampling rate.

Ultra-high-definition audio, or UHD Audio, uses a 24/96 configuration, or a 24-bit resolution with a 96 kHz sample rate.

The best way to show this work process is by using a hands-on approach, so let's get right into the optimization process!

Digital Audio Optimization: Work Process

The logical work process for optimizing a digital audio sample asset across hardware devices and using widely adopted open source content delivery platforms involves creating a 32-bit asset in Audacity and using a 44.1 kHz or a 48 kHz sampling rate, and then creating a baseline 16-bit uncompressed PCM format. You target 16-bit audio in this chapter, because all Android OS, Kindle, and HTML5 OS devices support 16-bit audio. If you're targeting HD audio platforms and devices, you can perform this work process using 24-bit audio.

Baseline PCM File: Something to Measure Against

The first thing that you want to do is establish the "baseline" file size that you will measure your asset compression against using each of the major digital audio file formats. Fortunately, there's an uncompressed file format called pulse-code modulation (PCM) that serves this purpose and provides you with an additional widely supported digital audio file format to use, if you need it, on any of the open publishing platforms (all of which will support PCM).

There is another important rationalization for exporting an uncompressed PCM baseline file, besides measuring compression against. When any of your compressed (lossy or lossless) assets are decompressed (decoded) into system memory, PCM represents a **memory footprint** that is needed to hold and play back the digital audio asset. So from a publishing and programming standpoint, you should also want to know how much **device memory** is needed to hold your application's digital audio assets. This should be calculated by adding up all of your PCM file sizes.

Open your **CH9.aud** project file and the **Stereo Track** drop-down menu, as shown in Figure 12-1. Select **Set Sample Format** and set it to 16-bit PCM, or 24-bit PCM if you're targeting HD Audio.

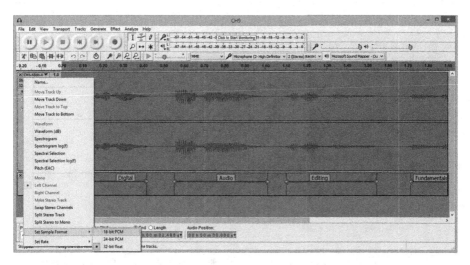

Figure 12-1. *Set Sample Format to 16-bit with Stereo Track menu*

The next step is to use the Audacity **File ➤ Export Audio** menu sequence to export a **WAV** file if you are on Windows, or an **AIFF** file if you are on Mac OS X (see Figure 12-2).

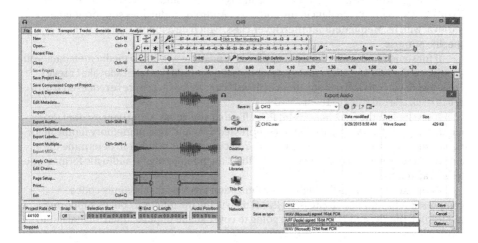

Figure 12-2. *Export baseline 16-bit PCM WAV or AIFF file format*

Once you click the **Save** button, the **Edit Metadata** dialog appears for you to enter any metadata that you want included in your audio file (see Figure 12-3). The data is stored in each file format along with the audio data and it can be accessed in Android. This dialog appears for each audio format's export.

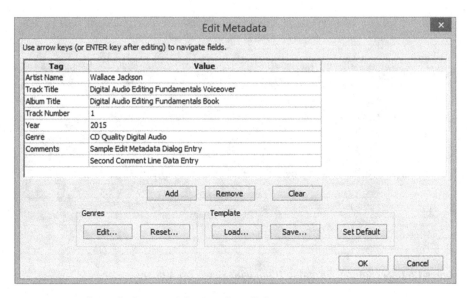

Figure 12-3. *The Audacity 2.1.1 Edit Metadata dialog*

If you are wondering how your applications will read and support audio metadata if you choose to install the data in the audio file, Android Studio does support metadata retrieval with its **MediaMetadataRetriever** class, which developers utilize for this very specific purpose.

If for some reason your Android application needs to use audio media metadata, you should use the Edit Metadata dialog along with the Android MediaMetadataRetriever class, which you can learn more about at developer.android.com/reference/android/media/MediaMetadataRetriever.html.

If you look at the CH12.wav 16-bit PCM file that you've saved out, you see that the file size is 428 KB. So your baseline uncompressed data and system memory footprint for a 2.48-second voice-over sample is 428 KB. You can use this number to determine the amount of compression that you will get with all the popular digital audio file formats you looked at in Chapter 4.

The next step is to go through the optimization process; that is, apply codec compression to your uncompressed (PCM) data using the different codecs supported in Android, Kindle, and HTML5. I am going to cover all the popular, open, digital audio formats.

Once that work process is completed, you are able to ascertain which resulting digital audio assets provide you with the highest quality digital audio playback in conjunctions with the lowest possible data footprint. Let's get right to it!

Exporting Lossless Audio: FLAC Audio Format

The first format that I am going to try out is the FLAC audio codec, because it uses lossless compression. This gives you a good idea of what kind of data footprint reduction you can get using compression, which does not throw away any of the original audio data. Using a lossless compression algorithm gives you as perfect a result as the 16-bit PCM WAV audio does! To do this, you'll again use the **File ➤ Export Audio** menu sequence. This time, you'll open the **Save as type** drop-down menu and select the **FLAC Files** format (see Figure 12-4).

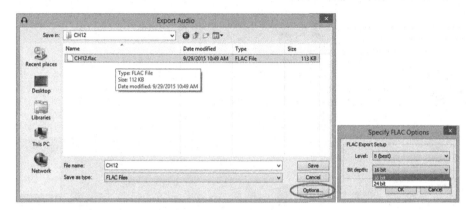

Figure 12-4. *Export Audio as FLAC format, in 16-bit at Level 8*

I named the file **CH12.flac** and saved it into my CH12 folder for this book. Notice that there are only FLAC files listed in the center area of the dialog. This is because now that you have selected the FLAC file format, this region in the dialog will only show FLAC files, and currently, there are none in the CH12 folder. Because I wanted to show file size for each format in Figure 12-4, I saved the file prior, so the size would be included in the screenshot, as well as the dialog settings and the options dialog (this way, I'm using only one screenshot rather than three).

To set the FLAC codec options, click the **Options** button and set the quality **Level** to 8 (best) and the **Bit depth** to use 16-bit data resolution. Note under the **Bit depth** drop-down that you can also use this FLAC codec for lossless, 24-bit HD audio. (I placed the **Export Audio** and **Specify FLAC Options** dialogs in one unified screen to save on the number of screenshots that I'm using.)

Once you've output the CH12.flac digital audio asset, go into the file manager to look at the file size, or use the **File ➤ Export Audio** menu sequence and mouse over **CH12.flac**. You see that it is 112 KB, reduced by more than 382%; 112 ÷ 428 = 0.261682, or only 26% as large as the PCM file was, or 100% - 26% = 74% less data. The 1/x (inverse) function on your calculator of 0.261682 gives you 3.82142857, an impressive 382.142857% data footprint reduction, with zero loss of data (quality). The FLAC format is good for use in Android Studio applications development, in conjunction with the PNG image format.

Next, let's take a look at the other open source digital audio file format, Ogg Vorbis, to see if it can provide an even smaller data footprint. Since Ogg Vorbis is a lossy file format, it should give you an even smaller file size than the FLAC codec.

Exporting Lossy Audio: Ogg Vorbis Audio Format

Again, use a **File ➤ Export Audio** work process to open the Export Audio dialog. Select the **Ogg Vorbis Files** option from the **Save as type** drop-down menu. I named the file **CH12**, which produces a CH12.ogg file name, and put it into the CH12 folder (see Figure 12-5). Click the **Options** button and select a **Quality** setting level between 0 and 10. I used the maximum setting of 10 to start with. During an actual data footprint optimization session, you will probably try several settings to see how the data footprint-to-quality trade-off is affected by the Quality slider setting.

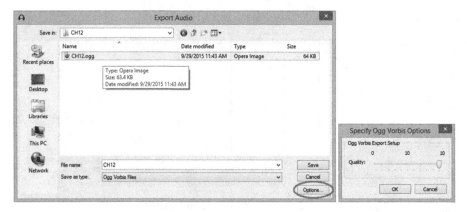

Figure 12-5. *Export Audio in Ogg Vorbis format at Quality of 10*

Once you have output a CH12.ogg audio asset, take a look at its file size. You see that it is 64 KB, reduced by 669% in file size; 64 KB ÷ 428KB = 0.14953, which is 15% of your baseline 428 KB. The inverse of this is 6.6875, or a 669% data reduction. This OGG file is 85% smaller than your PCM file.

Next, let's look at MP3, which is the most common lossy digital audio file format currently supported across publishing platforms. It should be quite interesting to see if MP3 can give you a smaller data footprint than the Ogg Vorbis codec.

Exporting Lossy MP3 Audio: MPEG3 Audio Format

Use you **File ➤ Export Audio** menu sequence again to bring up the Export Audio dialog. Set the **Save as type** drop-down selector to **MP3 Files** (see Figure 12-6). I named the file **CH12** and selected the **CH12 folder**. Then I clicked the **Options** button to open a **Specify MP3 Options** dialog (shown on the right in Figure 12-6). I used the maximum **Quality** bit-rate setting of 320 kbps, which is a high-quality setting for digital audio data. I am trying to get a high-end baseline for MP3 compression and still compare what MP3 can do against an uncompressed PCM baseline. I also selected the **Constant Bit Rate Mode**, because it is the easiest to decode, and a **Stereo Channel Mode**, since the file is currently in a Stereo Track configuration.

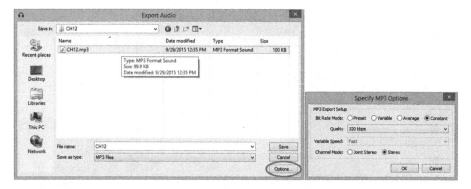

Figure 12-6. *Export Audio in MP3 format at Quality of 320 kbps*

If you like, you can also try different Quality Bit Rate settings and the Variable and Average Bit Rate Modes to see how they affect the MP3 data footprint. If you decide to do this, differentiate your files from each other; simply name the file with the settings type in the file name. For example, a file with a 320 kbps Quality setting and a Variable Bit Rate Mode should be named **CH12_320kbps_vbr.mp3**. This way, you can compare the audio file size of the MP3 and any other codec file format and do the simple math to figure out the percentage of the data footprint reduction relative to the different settings. You'll do this next for the CH12_320kbps_cbr.mp3 file.

The CH12.mp3 file size is 100 KB, representing a 428% data footprint reduction. To calculate this, 100 KB ÷ 428 KB = 0.233644859, which is 23% of the original, uncompressed file size; 100% − 23% = 77% file size reduction.

If you use your 1/x (inversion) key on a calculator, you can get a percentage reduction coming from the other direction by inverting 0.2336449, which gives you 4.28. This means that you reduced the file size by 4.28 times, which equates to a 428% reduction.

Now that you have seen that your MP3 file size is larger than the Ogg Vorbis, let's see how the MPEG4 AAC in M4A file format data compression can improve your file's size-to-quality ratio compared to MPEG3. Since MPEG4 is more recent and uses a more advanced codec algorithm, M4A should provide a better file size–to-quality optimization ratio than either Ogg Vorbis or MP3 codecs.

Exporting Lossy M4A Audio: MPEG4 Audio Format

Follow the usual **File ➤ Export Audio** work process to invoke the Export Audio dialog and select **M4A (AAC) Files (FFmpeg)** from the **Save as type** drop-down menu. If you did not install the LAME and FFMPEG libraries from Chapter 1, the file formats covered from here on out will not be available to you in Audacity 2.1. As usual, name the file **CH12**, which is named **CH12.m4a** by the Audacity Export Audio dialog after you click the **Options** button and open the **Specify AAC Options** dialog (see Figure 12-7). Click **OK** to set the maximum **Quality** of 500, and then click **Save** to save it in the CH12 directory. I'm betting that even using a Quality setting of 500, the MPEG-4 AAC codec is so advanced that it will give you a smaller file size than Ogg Vorbis did at 64 KB.

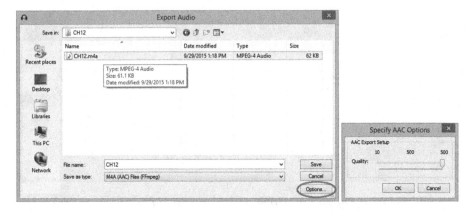

Figure 12-7. *Export Audio in M4A AAC format; set Quality to 500*

Your CH12.m4a file size is 62 KB, representing 14% of the uncompressed data footprint, giving an 86% reduction. To figure this out, 62 ÷ 428 is 0.1449, or 13% of your original, uncompressed file size; 100% – 14% = 86% file size reduction. Invert the 0.1449 and you get 6.9, or an impressive 690% data footprint reduction.

Now that you have seen that your M4A AAC file size is the most impressive data footprint reduction thus far, let's see if the much more specialized AMR-NB (Narrowband) data compression codec will give you any further data footprint improvements over MPEG4 AAC.

Since this codec is optimized for voice, chances are the results are going to be significantly better than any that you have encountered thus far—so hold onto your hat! One thing to note about recording voices is that it does not require stereo.

Exporting Narrowband Audio: MPEG4 AMR Format

Even though the MPEG4 AMR-NB (Adaptive Multi-Rate Narrowband) codec and data format was originally designed (optimized) specifically for use with voice recording applications. However, there may be some other applications, for example, short-burst sound effects, that might obtain reasonable, if not fantastic, results by using this codec. As you know, any codec is simply a complex, mathematical algorithm, implemented using software. It doesn't discriminate, so, the only way to really find out which codec will give you the best compression to quality result with any given asset is to run the original uncompressed audio data through the codec, and then see what happens, which is what you are seeing over the course of this chapter.

AMR-NB is supported in Kindle, Android OS, Tizen OS, iOS and popular open HTML5 OS platforms and HTML5 browser software, including Mozilla Firefox and Google Chrome. It is also used in Blackberry OS and QuickTime.

Follow the usual **File ➤ Export Audio** work process to invoke the Audacity Export File dialog. Select your **AMR (narrow band) Files (FFmpeg)** option from the **Save as type** drop-down menu. As usual, name the file **CH12**, which is named CH12.amr by the Exporter, after you click **Save**.

Save this file in your CH12 directory, or whatever your digital audio assets folder is named, and then click the **Options** button to open the **Specify AMR-NB Options** dialog (see Figure 12-8).

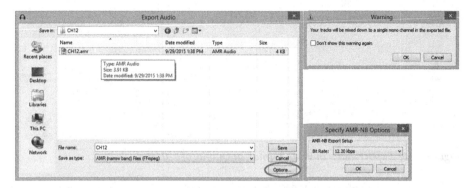

Figure 12-8. *Export Audio in AMR format; set Bit Rate to 12.20*

I chose to use the 12.20 kbps **Bit Rate** setting to initially get the maximum quality results possible with this codec. Later I can try other settings for comparison purposes and put together a results table to see which is best.

Click **Save** and you should get a **Warning** dialog (see Figure 12-8) informing you that your Stereo Track will be converted to a Mono Track. As you can see on the left of Figure 12-8, this is the smallest data footprint that you've obtained thus far, using only 4 KB of data.

Interestingly, when you play this AMR audio data sample, it still sounds a lot like the audio contained inside the other supported codec formats that you have generated thus far. The CH12.amr file size is 4 KB.

This represents more than a 99% data footprint reduction, some of which is from making a stereo data sample monoaural. To figure this out, 4 KB ÷ 428 KB = 0.00935. This is 0.94% of an original uncompressed file size; 100% − 1% = 99% file size reduction. If you invert 0.00934579, you get 107, which represents a 10,700% reduction in data footprint.

Exporting Audio for Windows: WMA Audio Format

Just in case you are delivering content on Windows OS, let's cover **WMA** or **Windows Media Audio**, which is supported by the Windows Media Player. The last three formats that you are exporting in this chapter use the FFMPEG library that you installed in Chapter 1. The WMA format also uses the library, shown in a drop-down selector using an **(FFmpeg)** denotation. Follow a **File ➤ Export Audio** work process to invoke the Export Audio dialog and select **WMA (Version 2) Files (FFmpeg)** from the **Save as type** drop-down menu. As usual, name this file **CH12**, which is named CH12.wma. Save it into your audio assets folder (mine is a CH12 directory), and then click the **Options** button to open the **Specify WMA Options** dialog (see Figure 12-9). I chose to initially set my **Bit Rate** setting at the highest, 320 kbps. Click **OK** to set **Quality**. Click **Save** to export your CH12.wma file.

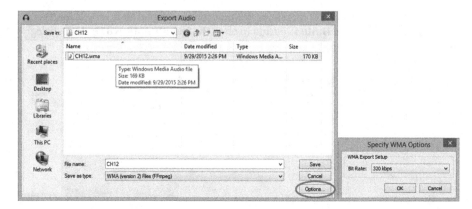

Figure 12-9. *Export Audio in WMA format, at Quality of 320 kbps*

The CH12.wma file size is 170 KB, representing 40% of the uncompressed data footprint and giving you a 60% data reduction.

To figure this out, 170 ÷ 428 = 0.3972, or 40% of your original, uncompressed file size; 100% – 40% = 60% file size reduction. Invert the 0.39719626 and you get 2.517647, or a not-so-impressive 252% data footprint reduction.

Now that you've seen that your WMA file size has the least impressive data footprint reduction thus far, let's fully compare all eight of the digital audio file formats that you generated. For my OS, it is the Windows Explorer file manager.

The Audio Codec Results: Spanning 4 KB to 400 KB

As you can see in Figure 12-10, I opened my CH12 folder in an operating system file management utility to get a comparison viewpoint of all of these digital audio files in one location.

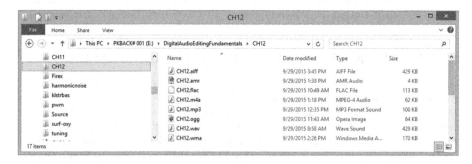

Figure 12-10. *Eight different exported digital audio formats*

The AMR-NB codec, which is optimized for voice and uses a Mono Track, is the clear winner at 4 KB—more than one hundred times less data used to reproduce the voice-over.

For Stereo Track usage, MPEG-4 AAC and the open sourced Ogg Vorbis codec virtually tie for second place at around 64 KB. They both have widespread support in Kindle, Android, and HTML5, just as AMR-NB does, and are appropriate for use in other types of digital audio, such as music and sound effects.

Tied for third place at around 100 KB each are the MP3, which is lossy, and the FLAC, which is lossless. Between the two, I would opt for using FLAC, although the playback support for MP3 is more widespread.

Finally, in last place is Windows Media Audio (WMA) with a 170 KB data footprint. You can use for Windows Media Player, but be advised that these other digital audio data formats also work in Windows applications. I'd opt for MPEG-4 or Ogg Vorbis.

I am not including the baseline 428 KB AIFF (Mac OS X), or WAV (Windows) digital audio formats in this analysis, but if a storage data footprint isn't an issue, they can be used with results as impressive as FLAC, as they give you a 100% quality reproduction of your digital audio sample data.

Summary

In this chapter, you looked at digital audio data footprint optimization concepts, principles, and techniques regarding eight primary digital audio formats, supported across all four of the key open new media content publishing platforms (HTML5, Android, Kindle, Java) that can decompress your digital audio assets created with Audacity 2.1.1.

You looked at how you should match the specifications for your digital audio assets to the hardware capabilities of your target hardware devices. For high-quality audio, this means using 24-bit 96 kHz audio for HD Audio devices or 16-bit 48 kHz audio to cover all mainstream audio hardware devices.

You learned how to use Audacity to export audio into six of the most widely utilized digital audio codec formats used in HTML5, Kindle, Java, and Android applications development today.

You learned how to calculate a data footprint reduction percentage, and applied this to the six different data formats to see a range of reductions from 60% to more than 99%, spanning FLAC, OGG, MP3, MPEG4, WMA, and AMR digital audio codecs.

In the next chapter, you learn about programming code to implement digital audio inside some of the most popular open source publishing platforms, including HTML5, Kindle, Android Studio, Java, and JavaFX.

CHAPTER 13

■ ■ ■

The Interactivity of Digital Audio: Programming

Now that you have learned how to create professional digital audio assets using the powerful features in Audacity 2.1 and you know how to export these assets to the most widely used audio file formats in popular content publishing platforms, it's time to take a look at application programming platforms. I am covering this in its own chapter in case you want to take your digital audio compositing career to the next level. In this chapter you will learn about the internal programming language used for Audacity, called **Nyquist**, as well as external programming languages that support digital audio, such as C# (.NET), Objective C (iOS), Java (Android Studio, Linux), JavaFX, JavaScript, HTML5, and CSS3 (WebKit browsers, and HTML5 operating systems).

This is important information to know if you plan to use digital audio samples in programming projects or in open software development platforms, or if you have any interest in learning more about adding programming.

The platforms run a majority of the consumer electronics devices, and include Java (Android Studio and WebKit), JavaFX (Android, iOS, Windows, Linux, Mac OS X, Solaris) and JavaScript with CSS3 and HTML5 scripting (WebKit browsers).

This chapter is not going to teach you programming, for that would take an number of books (and coding experience), but it will expose you to what's possible if you extend the journey you are on from digital audio compositing to new media software development. Everything covered in the chapter is free for commercial use. You can go and download Android Studio (IntelliJ), Java and JavaFX (NetBeans), HTML5 (NetBeans), and Nyquist (NyquistIDE).

Let's start with Nyquist, the programming language for Audacity, and then cover open platform languages such as Java (Android and Kindle), JavaScript (HTML5), and the JavaFX new media engine, which is now a part of Java 7, 8, and 9.

Audacity's Scripting Language: Nyquist 3

As you have seen already, Audacity 2.1 supports an internal scripting language for automating digital audio work processes. A scripting language is traditionally referred to in the computer industry as a **batch processing language**. This term comes from the old mainframe days

© Wallace Jackson 2015
W. Jackson, *Digital Audio Editing Fundamentals*, DOI 10.1007/978-1-4842-1648-4_13

when data was input during the day by employees, and then "batch processed" at night by computers while the employees got some sleep. I'll first cover how to install Nyquist and then we'll look at other languages that support digital audio compositing.

Downloading Nyquist: SourceForge.net Repository

You can download the NyquistIDE at SourceForge's open source software repository at `http://sourceforge.net/projects/nyquist/`.

Figure 13-1 shows Nyquist's project page on SourceForge.

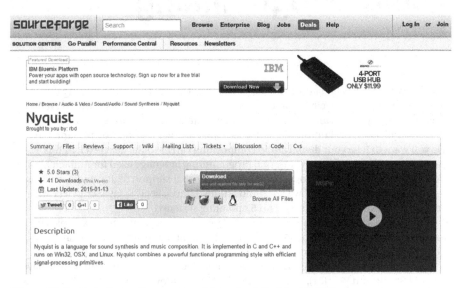

Figure 13-1. *Go to SourceForge.net and download the NyquistIDE*

After you install the NyquistIDE, let's look at the Nyquist scripting language and the integrated development environment (IDE) optimized for writing a Nyquist digital audio script.

Installing NyquistIDE: A Nyquist Integrated Editor

Download the Setup NyquistIDE Runtime version 3.05, which for Windows is named `setupnyqiderun305.exe`, to your hard disk drive. I have included this file in the ZIP archive for the book on the Apress repository, along with Nyquist documentation, and the half-dozen Nyquist plug-ins that you looked at in Chapter 11 as well. Right-click the EXE file and then select **Run As Administrator** from the context-sensitive menu. You get the **Welcome to NyquistIDE Setup Wizard** dialog, as shown in Figure 13-2. Next, accept the **License Agreement**, click **Next**, and accept the default destination location for the installation.

Figure 13-2. Start an install, accept license, and select folder

Click **Next** and then select your **Start Menu Folder**. Click **Next** to select the **Create a desktop icon** option. Click **Next** to get to the **Ready to Install** dialog (see Figure 13-3). Click the **Install** button to start the installation process.

Figure 13-3. Select Start Menu Folder, desktop icon, and Install

As you can see in Figure 13-4, you'll get the **Extracting** files progress bar, which tells you which Nyquist files are being installed to your hard disk drive. After this process has finished, you get an **Information** dialog, which informs you what each version of Nyquist 3.0 added, the current version being 3.05. After you have reviewed this, click **Next** and make sure that your **Launch NyquistIDE** check box is selected.

Figure 13-4. Extract Files, Read Information and Launch Nyquist

Once you click the **Finish** button, the NyquistIDE launches, and you see the integrated development environment shown in Figure 13-5. Select the **File ➤ Open** menu sequence. Use the **Open** dialog to select one of the Nyquist digital audio processing sample files from your C:\Program Files (x86)\Nyquist\demos folder. I selected the FFT demo because you looked at FFT data analysis in Chapter 9.

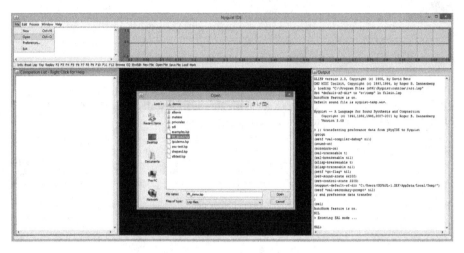

***Figure 13-5.** Launch the NyquistIDE to make sure that it is installed*

Like other popular IDE software, such as IntelliJ 14 for Android Studio, NetBeans 8.1 for HTML5, or Java and JavaFX, the NyquistIDE has a number of editor panes, output panes, digital audio data display panes, and so forth.

When you play with the NyquistIDE, you see that you can resize the panes and position them in any UI layout configuration that you feel comfortable working with. I placed the Completion List Pane on the left and the Output Pane on the right. Once you learn Nyquist, you can use it right inside of Audacity!

Nyquist code is quite compact; for instance, to multiply a signal with a generated carrier signal, you should use the following **LISP** command syntax:

```
( mult s ( hzosc 22050 ) )
```

You could also use the **SAL** programming language version:

```
return s * hzosc( 22050 )
```

Next, let's look at digital audio content delivery platforms, such as Android, Kindle, Java, and JavaScript.

Digital Audio Content Delivery Platforms

The Java (Android, JavaFX, and Kindle) and JavaScript (HTML5 and Kindle) programming languages support digital audio editing, compositing, effects, and playback. This covers many of the most popular platforms, including Android, Kindle, Blackberry, Linux OS, Tizen OS, Chrome OS, Firefox OS, Opera, HTML5 (WebKit), iOS, Open Solaris, and Windows 7, 8, and 10 OS.

Java and JavaFX API: javafx.scene.media Library

A digital audio compositing pipeline can be constructed and controlled by using Java 8 programming language code. Java has a library called **JavaFX**, which provides expansive new media assets support, spanning digital imaging, digital audio, digital video, and interactive 3D (i3D) real-time OpenGL ES 3 rendering. Many of the digital audio features and algorithms you have used in this book are in the **javafx.scene.media** library, which you will look at in this chapter. Java is used in Android, Kindle, HTML5, Windows, Mac OS X, Blackberry, Tizen, Linux, Unix, and Solaris. JavaFX apps can run on Android or iOS and gain support in Tizen, HTML5 and Blackberry. Thus Java, the world's most popular programming language, is truly a "code once, deliver everywhere" platform.

The Java AudioClip Class: Digital Audio Sequencing

JavaFX has an **AudioClip** class that can be used to create AudioClip objects in memory. An AudioClip object contains short data samples of audio that can be played with minimal latency. Long form audio, such as songs, use **Media**, **MediaPlayer**, and **MediaController** Java object types; one holds your media, one plays it from memory, and one provides a transport UI.

An AudioClip playback behavior is "fire it and forget it." Once the .play() method is called, the only operable control is to use the .stop() method. You can create and utilize your AudioClip object in Java with the following Java programming statement:

```
AudioClip myAudioClip = new AudioClip("http://serverhost/path/CH12.m4a");
myAudioClip.play();
```

AudioClips can be played multiple times, simultaneously. To accomplish the same task using a Media object, you would have to create a new MediaPlayer object for each audio sample played in parallel. Media objects are therefore better suited for long-playing sounds or entire audio performances, such as music.

The reason for this is that AudioClip objects store a raw, uncompressed (PCM) data sample in memory holding an entire digital audio sample, which is why I went into the work process that I did in Chapter 12.

This memory allocation can be quite large for long audio clips. A MediaPlayer object "streams" audio in and out of memory, to only have enough decompressed audio data pre-rolled in memory to play for a short amount of time.

This makes Media classes (and objects) much more memory efficient for long clips, especially if longer audio data streams need to be decompressed in real time using the CPU.

123

AudioClips are decompressed into memory at the time your application is loaded into memory on start-up, and thus do not use any CPU overhead during your application execution.

This makes the end-user experience much smoother, as the CPU can focus on your application programming logic, and not on streaming digital audio media, where it has to take your sample assets from your storage resource into memory and then into the hardware audio decoder to complete the audio playback cycle.

The Java AudioTrack Class: Digital Audio Compositing

A Java Media object asset might have multiple, parallel Tracks, such as a **VideoTrack** (object), a **SubtitleTrack** (object), and several **AudioTrack** objects, perhaps featuring different musical scores, or different narrator language translations, or both. The types of **Track** objects supported by an operating system may be inferred from the existing subclasses of the Track class, and currently include VideoTrack, AudioTrack, and SubtitleTrack.

Not all of your Media object assets contain each of these Track object types (Track subclasses). Additionally, the time span for a given Track object doesn't need to commensurate with the total time span for its containing Media object.

An AudioTrack class is a subclass (type of Track object) that describes a digital audio sample track. An audio track may be a component track in a digital music composition, for example, or one of several language translation tracks in an audiovisual Media object resource. The important thing to recognize is that these Track classes give you the same digital audio compositing capabilities that the Tracks menu provides in Audacity.

The significance of this (and what I am demonstrating in this chapter) is that you can take the digital audio editing and composition work process to the next level by making it interactive using open source development programming languages.

The Java AudioEqualizer Class: Digital Audio Frequency Control

The JavaFX **AudioEqualizer** class provides audio equalization controls for your JavaFX MediaPlayer objects, just like the EQ algorithm, which you applied to your digital audio sample assets in Audacity 2.1.

The AudioEqualizer class contains a Java Observable List that contains **EqualizerBand** elements. This EqualizerBand class provides encapsulation and attributes for each of your digital audio frequency bands within the AudioEqualizer object.

Each AudioEqualizer object instance is connected to the MediaPlayer object instance, and may be obtained using the MediaPlayer.getAudioEqualizer() method call. As you can see, Java is really advanced where digital audio editing and compositing API support is concerned, allowing you to bridge Audacity and Java.

Next, let's take a look at digital audio playback support implemented by using basic HTML5 markup language.

Using Digital Audio in HTML5: The <audio> Tag

The HTML5 content distribution platform features the <audio> tag for playing back digital audio assets. This tag is used in the following way inside HTML5 markup:

```
<audio controls>
  <source src="CH12.ogg" type="audio/ogg">
  <source src="CH12.mp3" type="audio/mpeg">
  <source src="CH12.wav" type="audio/wav">
  Please Note: Your browser does not support digital audio playback! Please
  upgrade to the latest version of your HTML5 browser or operating system.
</audio>
```

Using the controls attribute (parameter, flag, option) inside the opening <audio> tag adds digital audio playback (transport) user interface controls like the ones you see in Audacity. These include **Play**, **Pause**, **Position** (a shuttle slider), and **Volume**.

Multiple <source> elements can specify several different audio file formats. Your browser accesses these in the order they are specified, which is called the "fallback approach," and utilizes the first supported format. Currently, there are three supported digital audio file formats for the <audio> element: MPEG (MP3), pulse- code modulation (WAV), and the open source Ogg Vorbis (OGG) format. I specified Ogg Vorbis format first because it has the best quality and file size result. Then I fall back to a MP3 format, and finally to WAV for Windows Explorer users.

The type= parameter for the <source> child tag inside the parent <audio> tag specifies what is called a **MIME Type**.

MIME stands for **Multipurpose Internet Mail Extensions**, although MIME now extends to cover digital platform types beyond e-mail clients and servers.

It is important to note that the MIME types utilized for HTML5 web sites also need to be specified on the web server, so the multimedia types that you use in the application are defined up front.

The text content that you place between the <audio> and </audio> opening and closing digital audio tags display in browsers that do not support the <audio> element. Provide your users with an informative message that the ancient browser that they are using does not support digital audio playback, and ask them to upgrade to the latest HTML5 browser revision. I show this in the earlier sample code that so you can see how it is formatted.

Android Studio: Digital Audio Class and Interfaces

The Google Android platform is running more smartphones, e-book readers, tablets, iTVs, game consoles, smartwatches, and IoT (Internet of Things) devices, than any other OS platform on the planet. Apps are developed using Android Studio, under the IntelliJ 14 IDE. I've written a number of Pro Android titles for Apress over the past few years, including *Pro Android Graphics* (2013), *Pro Android UI* (2014), *Pro Android Wearables* (2015), *Pro Android IoT* (2016), and *Pro Java Games Development* (2016).

I cover how to code for the MediaPlayer, MediaController, or SoundPool digital audio classes in the *Pro Android UI* book.

The Android SoundPool Class: Digital Audio Sequencing Engine

The Android SoundPool class is similar to the JavaFX AudioClip class. Like the Android MediaPlayer class, it is part of the **android.media** package. It is also important to note that SoundPool objects spawned by the SoundPool class and MediaPlayer objects spawned by the MediaPlayer class can be utilized at the same time, if need be. In fact, there are distinct applications for both of these audio playback classes. As in JavaFX, MediaPlayer should be used for long-form audio (and video) data, such as albums, songs, audio books, or movies. SoundPool is best used for short-form audio snippets, especially when they need to be played in rapid succession and (or) combined, such as in a game, e-book, user interface design, or other gamified multimedia application.

Your SoundPool collection of audio samples can be loaded into memory from one of two places. The most common place is from inside your APK file, which I call "captive" new media assets, as they are inside your **A**ndroid **P**ac**K**age (APK).

In this case, assets live in your **/res/raw** project resource folder, as this is where digital audio assets go in an Android Studio project. The second place that samples are loaded from is an SD card or a similar storage location. This is what you would term your Android OS file system.

SoundPool uses the Android MediaPlayer Service to decode the audio asset into memory. It does this by using uncompressed 16-bit PCM (Mono or Stereo) audio. This is the main reason that I've been teaching you a work process that optimizes the audio using 16-bit sampling resolution, because if you utilize 8-bit, Android upsamples that audio into 16-bit, and you end up with wasted data that could have received better quality.

This means that if you are targeting Android Studio applications, you should optimize for sample frequency, but not for sample resolution (use 16-bit). Do not use Stereo audio unless you absolutely need to, as it will double the memory footprint used for each sample.

To get the optimal result across the largest number of consumer electronics devices, it's important to conform your optimization work process to how Android SoundPool works. Thus, 48 kHz is the best sample frequency to use if possible, with 44.1 kHz coming in a close second. You used 44.1 kHz in Audacity because that's the default setting (44.1 kHz 32-bit sample resolution).

To optimize, keep your sample short, remove all unneeded noise, trim unnecessary pre- and post-sample data, and use Mono, just as I taught you over the course of this book. Then use a modern codec—such as MPEG-4 AAC, Ogg Vorbis, or FLAC—to retain most of the quality while still culling a reasonable amount of digital audio data compression in your APK file. Calculate memory use with a raw uncompressed PCM (WAV or AIFF) audio file size.

When the SoundPool object is constructed in Java, you'll specify a **maxStreams** parameter by using an integer value. This parameter determines the number of digital audio streams that will be composited, or rendered, in memory at the same time. Be sure to set this important parameter precisely, as it sets aside memory.

Setting the maximum number of streams parameter as a small number, if possible, is a good standard practice. This is because doing so helps to **minimize CPU cycles** used for processing audio samples. This reduces any likelihood that the SoundPool audio sequencing engine will affect any of those other areas of your application performance (CPU processor usage).

A SoundPool engine tracks the number of active audio streams (data samples) to make sure that it does not exceed the maxStreams setting. If the maximum number of audio streams has been exceeded, SoundPool aborts the previously playing streams. SoundPool does this based upon a **sample priority value**, which you can specify to control which sample's playback stops first.

If SoundPool finds two (or more) digital audio samples that have an equal sample priority value, it makes a decision on which sample to stop playing, based solely on sample age, which means the sample that has been playing the longest is the one that is terminated (playback is stopped). I like to call this the "Logan's Run principle."

Priority level values are set using low to high numeric values. This means that higher (larger) numbers represent the higher priority levels. Priority is evaluated when any call to SoundPool's .play() method causes a number of active streams to exceed the maxStreams value, which is set when the SoundPool object is instantiated (created in memory using a new keyword).

When the sample priority for the new stream is lower than all of the active streams, the new sound will not play, and the .play() function returns a stream ID of 0. For this reason, be sure that the application's Java code keeps track of exactly what's going on with the audio sample's priority-level settings.

Samples can be **looped** in SoundPool by setting a non-zero looping value. The exception to this is that a value of –1 causes samples to loop forever, and under this circumstance, the application code must make a call to a SoundPool .stop() method to stop the infinitely looping sample.

So non-zero integer values cause a sample to repeat itself that specified number of times; thus, a value of 7 will cause your sample to play back a total of eight times, as computers start counting using the number 0 instead of the number 1.

The sample playback rate can be changed using SoundPool, which as mentioned, makes this class a part of your **audio synthesis** tool as well. A sample playback rate of 1 causes your sample to play at the original frequency. A sample playback rate of 2 causes your sample to play at twice its original frequency, which shifts it up a full octave higher if it is a musical instrument note.

Similarly, a sample playback rate set to 0.5 causes SoundPool to play the sample at half of its original frequency, which then sounds like the note is a full octave lower.

The sample playback-rate range of SoundPool is currently limited to 0.5 to 2.0; however, this may be upgraded in a future API revision to 0.25 to 4, which gives a developer a four-octave sample playback range.

Now it's time to learn about a couple of the other audio-related classes in Android Studio. As you can see, I'm trying to cover as many key Android digital audio classes in this book as is humanly possible!

The Android AudioTrack Class: Digital Audio Compositing

Just like JavaFX, the Android OS has its own AudioTrack class, which allows you to composite digital audio using Tracks, as you do in Audacity. The AudioTrack class manages and plays a single audio resource for Android application development purposes. It allows streaming of PCM audio buffers to Android's digital audio "sink" for layered playback, if more than one AudioTrack object is implemented.

AudioTrack instances can operate under two modes: **static** and **streaming**. In the streaming mode, your application writes a continuous stream of data to an AudioTrack object. This is done by using one of this class's .write() methods. A streaming mode is useful when playing blocks of audio data that are too big to fit in memory because of the duration of the sample, or that too big to fit in memory because of the audio data characteristics (a high sampling rate or sample resolution, or both), or the digital audio sample is received (or synthesized) while previously queued digital audio samples are playing.

The static mode should be chosen when dealing with short sounds that fit into memory and that need to be played with the minimum amount of latency. This static mode should be the preferential mode for user interface feedback or game audio that is triggered frequently by the end user. It's important to note that a SoundPool class may do the same thing with far more memory efficiency, as well as with other features, such as pitch shifting.

Upon instantiation (at the time of creation), your AudioTrack object initializes its associated **audio buffer**. The size of this audio buffer is specified during object construction; it determines how long your AudioTrack can play before running out of memory allocation (space) to hold the audio sample data. For an AudioTrack that is using a static mode, this size is the maximum size of the sound that can be played from it. For the streaming mode, audio data is transferred to the audio sink using data chunks in sizes less than or equal to the total audio data buffer size specification.

Next, let's take a look at MediaPlayer and MediaRecorder classes for long-form audio playback and recording audio and video data streams.

The Android MediaPlayer Class: Digital Audio Playback

Also like Java and JavaFX, Android has a MediaPlayer class that can be used to play long-form audio and video media assets. The MediaPlayer is a complete player solution featuring a transport user interface and all controls necessary to play, stop, seek, reset, or pause new media assets such as digital audio or video.

This MediaPlayer class has a major amount of information attached to it in a programming scenario; the topic warrants an entire book. If you want to learn more about it, try the books *Android Apps for Absolute Beginners* (Apress, 2014) or *Pro Android UI* (Apress, 2014), or visit the Android Developer web site at http://developer.android.com/reference/android/media/MediaPlayer.html.

Let's take a look at some Java statements needed to create a URL String, instantiate a new **myMediaPlayer** object, set an audio stream type and data source, and go through the **states** associated with an digital audio asset **playback cycle**, including asset preparation, playback (start), pause, stop, reset, remove from memory (release), and nullification, as outlined here:

```
String url = "http://server-address/folder/file-name"; // Audio Asset URL
MediaPlayer myMediaPlayer = new MediaPlayer();
myMediaPlayer.setAudioStreamType(AudioManager.STREAM_MUSIC);
myMediaPlayer.setDataSource(url);
```

```
myMediaPlayer.prepare();      // Prepare Audio Asset (buffer from server)
myMediaPlayer.start();        // Start Playback
myMediaPlayer.pause();        // Pause Playback
myMediaPlayer.stop();         // Stop Playback
myMediaPlayer.reset();        // Reset MediaPlayer object
myMediaPlayer.release(); //   Remove MediaPlayer object from memory
myMediaPlayer = null;    //    Nullify your MediaPlayer object
```

In Android Studio, this Java code creates a **String** object to hold the digital audio asset URL (line one). It declares and instantiates a **MediaPlayer** object (line two). It sets an **AudioStreamType** object using the **STREAM_MUSIC** constant from the **AudioManager** class (line three). It sets the **DataSource** object, the value of your String object (line four). Lines 5 through 11 go through the digital audio asset playback cycle states of preparations (loading into memory), playback start, playback pausing (if needed), playback halting (stop), playback reset, playback release (removing from memory), and object clearing to a null or unutilized state.

If you want to learn Java, check out the *Beginning Java 8 Games Development* (Apress, 2015); it covers Java programming in the context of new media assets, including digital audio.

MediaPlayer plays digital audio and digital video assets, usually in long form (several minutes), which were created and optimized outside of Java or Android using professional software like Audacity 2.1. For digital video editing, you can use the EditShare Lightworks open source software, which you can download at http://www.lwks.com.

The Android MediaRecorder Class: Digital Audio Recording

Unlike Java and JavaFX, Android has its own MediaRecorder class, probably because Android phones have built-in cameras. (Android also has its own Camera (and Camera2) API to control the camera hardware.) The MediaRecorder class can be used to record long-form audio and video, and thus to create new media assets.

The MediaRecorder is a complete media recorder solution, featuring all the controls necessary to start, stop, reset, and release multimedia recording hardware devices.

Let's take a look at some Java statements needed to declare a MediaRecorder object, named **myMediaRecorder**. Use a Java **new** keyword to instantiate this object using a constructor method called **MediaRecorder()**. Set your **AudioSource** constant to **MIC**. Set the **OutputFormat** and **AudioEncoder** constants to **AMR_NB**. Set the **OutputFile** object reference and go through the recording **states** associated with a digital audio data **recording lifecycle**, including memory preparation, start recording, stop recording, and removing a data capture area from memory. All of this is outlined here:

```
MediaRecorder myRecorder;
myRecorder = new MediaRecorder();
myRecorder.setAudioSource(MediaRecorder.AudioSource.MIC);
myRecorder.setOutputFormat(MediaRecorder.OutputFormat.AMR_NB);
myRecorder.setAudioEncoder(MediaRecorder.AudioEncoder.AMR_NB);
myRecorder.setOutputFile(PATH_AND_FILE_NAME_REFERENCE);
```

```
myRecorder.prepare();    // This sets aside system memory for recording
myRecorder.start();      //  This starts the camera hardware recording
myRecorder.stop();       // This stops the camera hardware from recording
myRecorder.reset();      //  You can reuse a reset MediaRecorder object
myRecorder.release();  // Once released a MediaRecorder object can't be used
```

The MediaRecorder class has a huge amount of information attached to using it in a programming scenario; the topic could have an entire book written on it. If you want to learn more about it, visit the Android Developer web site at http://developer.android.com/reference/android/media/MediaRecorder.html.

Summary

In this chapter, you learned about topics that relate to digital audio programming and the programming languages used in digital editing software and app development software. The final chapter in this book covers publishing platforms.

CHAPTER 14

■ ■ ■

Publishing Digital Audio: Content Delivery Platforms

Now that you have an understanding of the fundamental concepts, terms, and principles behind digital audio editing, compositing, and programming, it is time to look at how digital audio is published on popular open source publishing platforms. I am going to delineate this chapter using **consumer electronics genres**, as these define the different types of applications.

For example, **e-book readers**, or e-readers, such as the Kindle Fire, use Kindle KF8 e-books. Smartwatches use Android Wear SDK under the Android Studio 1.4 and using the Android OS 5.4 API.

iTVs use the Android TV SDK in Android Studio 1.4 with the Android OS 5.4 API.

Automobile dashboards use the Android Auto SDK with the Android Studio 1.4 IDE and the Android OS 5.4 API.

Tablets and smartphones use Android SDK in Android Studio 1.4 IDE with the Android OS 5.4 API.

Laptops and netbooks use Java with JavaFX. These hardware devices support all the open industry-publishing standards, such as PDF, HTML5, and EPUB3, as well as "closed" (not open source) operating systems like Windows and iOS.

iOS runs on the Apple Watch and there is supposed to be Apple TV. iOS also runs on the iPhone and iPad.

Microsoft purchased Nokia, so these smartphones also run Windows. However, all the other major manufacturers in the world use open Android and HTML5 operating systems and platforms, so that is what I will focus on.

You'll continue to look at how to publish on electronic hardware devices using the software development platforms that these devices support, including Kindle KF8, EPUB3, Android Studio 1.4 (Android OS 5.4), Java, JavaFX, PDF, HTML5, CSS3, and JavaScript, many of which were covered in Chapter 13.

© Wallace Jackson 2015

W. Jackson, *Digital Audio Editing Fundamentals*, DOI 10.1007/978-1-4842-1648-4_14

Open Source Formats: PDF, HTML, and EPUB

Let's start with the content publishing formats that support digital audio and that have been defined by industry groups, such as **EPUB** and **HTML**, or that have been "open sourced," such as the Adobe **Portable Document Format**, or **PDF**. These formats support a wide range of digital audio file formats. I'm starting with the open formats because they are usable across every type of hardware device covered in this chapter. I'll start with platforms with the widest support.

Portable Document Format: Digital Audio in PDF

The Adobe PDF format is utilized by the Adobe Acrobat Reader, which is used around the world for publishing rich media documents that can include digital audio, digital video, and i3D (interactive 3D). Acrobat Reader is free and the PDF format is open source, but the Adobe Acrobat Professional series of publishing tools are paid software packages—and worth the money if you need to publish via this widely accepted publishing format.

The PDF format supports two digital audio formats, MP3 and MPEG-4 AAC LC; the best option is MPEG-4 AAC LC, as far as the quality-to–file size ratio is concerned. This is because the audio encoding algorithm is more recent, and therefore, much more advanced mathematically. As you saw in Chapter 12, MPEG4 AAC LC gets you far better data footprint results than MP3, so use MPEG4 AAC LC encoding whenever possible for the digital audio assets in your projects.

It used to be that a PDF was only used for creating business documents. However, it has been adopted for e-book formats; in fact, you might be reading my books using the PDF format. Other e-book formats include Kindle (MOBI) and EPUB (EPUB3), which are also covered in this chapter.

Another advantage of the PDF format is that it offers **digital rights management** (DRM) support. This allows you to copy-protect (lock) your document if you want to sell it. Adobe has a PDF Server product that incorporates this DRM feature and allows you to better market PDF content.

It's rumored that the other two publishing formats covered in this section of the chapter are also looking at adding DRM support in the future. Let's look at HTML5 next.

HyperText Markup Language: HTML5 Digital Audio

You already know how to use the `<audio>` tag from Chapter 13; thus, you know that HTML5 supports three digital audio formats—MP3, Ogg Vorbis, and PCM WAVE. The best is Ogg Vorbis, as far as the quality-to–file size ratio is concerned. As you saw in Chapter 12, Ogg Vorbis rivals MPEG4 AAC. This is quite impressive for an open format.

It used to be that HTML5 was only used for creating web site designs, until web browser manufacturers decided to utilize their browser code to create HTML5 operating systems for consumer electronics devices, given the success of Android, Bada, and iOS.

Putting this browser code, with **app launch icon** support, on top of the Linux kernel, produced the Chrome OS (Motorola), Firefox OS (Panasonic iTV), and Opera OS (Sony Bravia iTVs).

There's also the Tizen OS (Samsung), which is based on a Linux OS created by Linus Torvald. It also uses HTML5. Tizen OS is managed by The Linux Foundation. HTML5 is easy to implement, thanks to an open source WebKit API that is also available in Android Studio 1.4 (Android OS 5.4).

HTML5 application and web site publishing is an excellent way to deliver content across all embedded mobile OS, desktop, and web browser platforms. This is why DRM is the future of HTML5 and why I showed you how to implement digital audio assets by using the **<audio control>** method.

Next, let's take a closer look at the open source EPUB 3 publishing standard, used for e-books, and soon for much more.

Electronic Publishing: Digital Audio in EPUB3

The EPUB specification is a distribution and interchange format standard for digital publications and documents. EPUB 3, the third major release of the open EPUB standard, consists of four specifications, each defining an important component of an overall EPUB document. **EPUB Publications 3** defines publication-level semantics, as well as conformance requirements for EPUB 3 documents. **EPUB Content Documents 3** defines XHTML, SVG, and CSS3 profiles for use in the context of your EPUB 3.0 publications. **EPUB Open Container Format 3.0**, or OCF3, defines a file format and is a processing model for encapsulating sets of related resource assets in one ZIP file format (EPUB Open Container). **EPUB Media Overlays 3.0** defines a format and a processing model for the data synchronization of text with digital audio assets.

EPUB 3.0 has been widely adopted as a format for digital books, also popularly known as **e-books**. The 3.0 specification significantly increased the EPUB format's capability, so it is capable of supporting a range of new media publication requirements. These include complex layout, new media and interactivity, and international typography (fonts) support.

The hope is that EPUB 3 will be utilized for a broad range of content, including books, magazines, and educational, professional, and scientific publications.

EPUB 3 supports audio (and video) embedded in documents by using the HTML5 <audio> tag (and <video> tag) elements. They inherit the same functions and feature set that these tags provide in HTML5. EPUB 3 supports MP3 audio as well as MPEG-4 AAC LC in an .m4a container (extension).

Another impressive new media feature in EPUB 3 is called **Media Overlay Documents**. If pre-recorded narration is available for your multimedia publication, such as what you've created in this book, these Media Overlay Documents offer the ability to synchronize your digital audio samples with the text inside the publishing content document (EPUB3 publishing platforms).

Open Platforms: Java, Android, and Kindle

The next set of formats that I am going to cover are open source and free for commercial use, but do not run across all hardware devices and are not industry specific, but instead are owned by major industry hardware and software manufacturers. Oracle owns Java and JavaFX; Google owns Android; and Amazon owns Kindle (MOBI) and Kindle Fire, which uses the KF8 format. Let's cover these based on the genres or types of consumer electronics devices that run on these formats, starting with e-book readers, since the three formats just covered are all widely used for delivering e-books as well (as you can see on the Apress web site when you purchase their titles).

e-Book Readers: Kindle Fire, Android, Java, and PDF

The e-book reader hardware device is actually an Android tablet, which is why I included Android in the header of this section. The world's most popular e-book reader, the Kindle Fire, runs on Android OS, as does the Sony e-book reader, and the Barnes & Noble NOOK e-book reader. Even the Apple iPad runs Kindle, EPUB3 and PDF e-book titles; so do Blackberry tablets and Microsoft Surface tablets. The reason that I included Java in the headers is because Kindle has Java capabilities for interactive e-books, and Android uses Java. Since e-book readers also read PDF files, I included PDF in the header.

Because most e-book readers are actually Android tablets or iPads, there are a large number of platforms; you saw the key open ones in Chapter 13 to develop digital audio content with.

This means that you can deliver a digital audio content and user experience through an Android application, an HTML5 application, a JavaFX application, an HTML5 web site, a Kindle 8 e-book, an EPUB3 e-book, a NOOK e-book, or an interactive new media PDF document. This gives you a ton of flexibility for publishing audio to e-book readers.

Since this is all done using Java, JavaFX, Android Studio, and the HTML5 <audio> tag, the basics of how this is accomplished was covered in Chapter 13.

iTVs: Android TV, Java, JavaScript, and HTML5

The iTV, or interactive television set, is the most recent consumer electronics device to hit the marketplace. iTV devices are expected to explode in sales in 2016 and 2017. This is the reason that Google has developed a specialized version of Android SDK (software development kit) for iTVs called the **Android TV API** (application programming interface).

There are **HTML5 OS iTV** products available from Samsung (Tizen OS), Panasonic (Firefox OS), and Sony (Opera OS). So the iTV consumer electronic device is much like an e-book reader in that it allows you to create and deliver digital audio content by using Java or JavaFX (Android OS or HTML5 OS), HTML5 markup, CSS3, and JavaScript (iOS, Android OS, HTML5 OS).

An important feature that iTVs will have is high-quality digital audio reproduction. Manufacturers realize their iTV products will be installed in home theaters and living rooms, where elaborate sound systems are likely attached to the iTV using **SPDIF** digital audio or **stereo RCA** ports located on the rear of the iTV device.

It's also important to realize that with iTVs, your viewers will pay closer attention to content streams, both audio and video. This is not always the case on devices such as smartphones and automobile dashboards.

If you want to deliver digital audio content across all the iTV platforms, you should use HTML5. Android and iOS support HTML5, but HTML5 OS and web sites do not support Android and iOS applications. The other side of the decision is that Apple and

Google Play have more advanced app stores, so if you are going to monetize your digital audio content, you should consider developing apps with Java (Android) or JavaFX (iOS) more than using JavaScript under HTML5 operating systems and HTML5 browsers.

Smartwatch: Android WEAR, Java, and HTML5

The **smartwatch** is another consumer electronics device that recently hit the market. Smartwatch devices are also expected to explode in sales in 2016 and 2017, primarily because there are hundreds of manufacturers manufacturing them. The densely populated watch industry is moving to release smartwatch products so that they do not lose market share to consumer electronics manufacturers, such as LGE, Sony, Motorola, and Samsung, who already have several smartwatch products. One of the first custom Android APIs that Google developed was the **Android WEAR** with its **Watch Faces API**.

Digital audio is a very important feature that the smartwatch devices support, because 16-bit, 48 kHz audio is built into the hardware, and more importantly, because there is a massive high-end Bluetooth audio headphones market.

What this means is that the smartwatch product is like a MP3 player for your wrist: it doesn't require much screen-display real estate and it can provide a professional audio playback results. This is significant for digital audio producers and digital audio application developers.

Another important feature of smartwatches is that you'll be able to combine your digital audio assets with other highly functional attributes, such as time, date, weather, fashion, and health (especially fitness and physical health monitoring features like heart and pulse rate) hardware input.

Once smartwatch screen resolutions increase from 320 pixels to 480, 640, or 800 pixels, even more functionality becomes available to developers. The Huawei smartwatch already features a 400×400–pixel screen. So, high-resolution smartwatches should appear in 2016 or 2017, given that smartphones have 4K screens that are only 5 to 7 inches. An 800-pixel smartwatch screen is certainly possible, because the technology already exists.

As long as your smartwatch users have quality, Bluetooth headphones, and as long as you process and optimize your 16-bit 48 kHz digital audio assets perfectly, and use the lossless FLAC codec or high-quality settings for the Ogg Vorbis or MPEG-4 AAC codecs, you should rock the socks off your customers!

Auto Dashboard: Android AUTO, Java, and HTML5

The **automobile dashboard** is another recent consumer electronics device to hit the mass market. Auto dashboard devices are expected to become standard in cars by 2016 or 2017. A number of manufacturers already have them as standard equipment and all of the automobile manufacturers have signed on with Google to support Android AUTO, the custom Android SDK for automobile dashboard applications. Automobiles are a hyper-completive industry not likely to be left behind as far as technology is concerned, so it is a logical market for Android and HTML5 operating systems to get into.

Digital audio is a very important feature for auto dashboards to support, because extensive (and expensive) ultra-high quality audio playback hardware is often built right into the body of an automobile, especially in more expensive brands, which are almost half of the automobile brands on the market.

Digital audio is also the best fit for Android AUTO apps, because there are stringent guidelines regarding tasking driver attention off the road. The digital audio Android AUTO apps do not require the user to look at any display screen, and are thus the safest type and should pass muster in the Google Play Automotive App section of the online store.

There are entirely new consumer electronic device types that thus far have very few apps, especially digital audio apps, so the opportunity for audio developers is nothing short of immense. So make some big money!

Smartphones and Tablets: Android, Java, and HTML5

Smartphones or **tablets** have been around a while, as has the hybrid between the two, commonly referred to as a **phablet**. The Android OS covers all of these device types, as well as personal computers that run the Android OS. There are billions of smartphones and tablets, and nearly a hundred consumer electronics manufacturers making products for the open source Android platform. For this reason, it is an amazing opportunity for audio content and applications, as there are not as many digital audio-centric applications as there are video-centric or imaging (visually oriented) applications.

Since smartphones and tables have been on the market for a while, they are most likely to upgrade their 16-bit 48 kHz CD audio hardware support to 24-bit HD digital audio hardware. And since Android supports the 24-bit FLAC codec, pristine digital sample audio is within the reach of digital audio editors and compositors.

iTVs are also likely to include 24-bit HD Audio support, as customers will demand HD Audio and SPDIF connectors for their UHD home theater installations. In fact, there are already UHD iTV products. I would be quite surprised if these did not already feature HD Audio hardware. Again, a bright future awaits audio editors, as CD- and HD-quality digital audio apps are still rare in the market.

Game Consoles: Android, Java, JavaFX, and HTML5

Since Android, Java, JavaFX, and HTML5 now support **OpenGL ES 3.1**, a plethora of advanced game console products have appeared, affordably priced between $50 and $100. This is yet another opportunity waiting for digital audio editing gurus, which you'll soon be, once you practice what you've learned in this book. These consoles run on Android and therefore support Java and HTML5, as well as JavaFX apps or Android applications, and even e-books, for that matter. There are more than a dozen brands available now.

Some major industry brands (manufacturers) are producing game controllers with Android computers inside, for instance an NVIDIA SHIELD or GameStick. Other major manufacturers, such as Amazon, manufacture a game-console iTV hybrid product, such as the Amazon Fire TV. Others, such as OUYA and GamePop, make STB (set-top box) products that game controllers (and iTVs) plug into. Some, such as OUYA and Razer ForgeTV, come with both the STB and the game controller, for a complete gaming package.

Since all of these game controllers support Android, you can utilize the audio formats covered in this book, and if you use HTML5 or EPUB3, you can use Ogg Vorbis, MP3, or MPEG4 AAC—all of which provide good results. (I covered the code for doing this in Chapter 13.)

Future Devices: Robots, VR, and Home Appliances

The future of Android SDKs will surely bring more custom APIs. I expect to see **Android VR** for virtual reality goggles, as well as **Android HOME** for home appliances or home control units, and maybe even an **Android ROBOT** SDK for Android-based robots. I have already seen many of these products in the marketplace for some time, so it's up to Google to provide custom APIs for these product genres, all of which will be great audio app platforms for digital audio editors, multimedia producers, and developers.

Audio will be an important component for all of these devices. I expect at least two of these genres, home appliances and virtual reality, to support HD audio to increase the user experience level (virtual reality), and because home theaters use HD Audio (home appliances and control units). Robots will probably stick with 16-bit 48 kHz audio, as that is enough bandwidth to produce professional results. So if you follow the work processes outlined in this book, you should be able to produce pristine results, especially if you use FLAC codec at a 16-bit sample resolution and a 48 kHz sampling rate.

Paid Software Platforms: iOS or Windows

The last section of this chapter covers formats that are not open source; that is, they involve paid software. Paid hardware is required to develop Apple platforms. Some formats require the company that owns the platform to approve your app before it can be sold in the app store. It is important to note that you are able to get around this approval process by developing with HTML5 for these platforms, or by using JavaFX; therefore, you can still deliver content for your clients without having to invest thousands of dollars in hardware (for iOS) and software (Windows Visual C++ or C# software development packages).

Apple iPhone and iPad: Supported Audio Formats

The Apple iPhone and iPad run iOS and support the following audio formats, many of which are covered in this book: MPEG-4 AAC (16 to 320 Kbps), AIFF, AAC Protected (MPEG-4 DRM format in the iTunes Store), MP3 (CBR 16 to 320 Kbps), MP3 VBR, Windows WAV PCM, and the proprietary Apple Lossless and Audible formats (V2 through V4). Apple QuickTime is also proprietary, and so the MPEG-4 and WebM video formats are far more widespread in use for this reason.

Other closed or paid formats, like Flash and PowerPoint, have suffered the same fate: replaced with open, free-for-commercial use formats such as Java, HTML5, and EPUB3.This is why I have focused primarily on the open sourced digital audio codecs and formats, or those like MPEG-4, which are licensed for use in JavaFX, Android Studio, and HTML5.

Windows Phone: Supported Digital Audio Formats

The Windows Phone 8 supports the following audio formats (covered in the book): MPEG-3, WMA Standard 9.2, WMA Pro, MPEG-4 AMR-NB, and MPEG-4 AAC LC. The Windows 7, 8.1 and 10 operating systems also support these formats. If you are developing for your corporate clients running Windows 10, use the WMA Pro codec, as it probably has the best codec algorithms and HD Audio support.

Summary

In this final chapter, you looked at the digital audio publishing concepts, principles, and file formats used to compress and decompress digital audio assets, as well as to publish and distribute them to your end users. You also looked at many of the different formats, platforms, and devices available to you for developing digital audio content.

I hope that you have enjoyed this journey through digital audio editing, compositing, programming, and publishing concepts and work processes, and that you now have fundamental knowledge of digital audio, which you can build on in your new media design, multimedia development, and content publishing endeavors. Keep an eye out for my other books, covering Android Studio, Java and JavaFX, HTML5, and other new media genres, such as digital illustration and digital image compositing.

Index

© Wallace Jackson 2015

W. Jackson, *Digital Audio Editing Fundamentals*, DOI 10.1007/978-1-4842-1648-4

Printed in the United States
By Bookmasters